COFFINS, CATS AND
FAIR TRADE SEX TOYS

A Quick Brown Fox Publications Book

First published in Great Britain by Quick Brown Fox Publications in
February 2009; second edition published by
Quick Brown Fox Publications in March 2009.
Copyright © Jeremy Piercy 2009.
Edited by Adam Kirkman.
Contributing Editor Nick Witt.

ISBN-10 0955480485 ISBN-13 9780955480485

Cover design by Mandy Norman. Used with permission.

Quick Brown Fox Publications is an independent publisher. They want
to hear from first time authors so please get in touch. They'd love to hear
from you. Please recommend this book to a friend.

www.quickbrownfoxpublications.co.uk

This book is printed and bound in Great Britain by Print On Demand
Worldwide. This book is made from FSC accredited paper. The printing
process has been carbon offset and vegetable dyes were used. For more
details on their environmental printing policy, please visit their website,
www.printondemand-worldwide.com.

Mixed Sources
Product group from well-managed
forests, and other controlled sources
www.fsc.org Cert no. TT-COC-002641
© 1996 Forest Stewardship Council

FSC

The paper used for this book is FSC-certified and totally
chlorine-free. FSC (the Forest Stewardship Council) is
an international network to promote responsible
management of the world's forests.

www.jeremypiercy.co.uk
www.sharedearth.co.uk

COFFINS, CATS AND FAIR TRADE SEX TOYS

JEREMY PIERCY

QUICK BROWN FOX PUBLICATIONS, 2009

Contents

Foreword by Antony Worrall Thompson

IS THERE ANYTHING better than a beautifully cooked, healthy and delicious meal? For me, it can only be a beautifully cooked, healthy and delicious meal that *improves our planet*. The growth of fair trade food has been well documented, but that's really only the tip of the iceberg-lettuce: the aim of fair trade is to change our planet for the better.

I've supported fair trade for many years through my recipes, various endorsements and campaign for organic foods. My family history also plays some part in why I'm supporting fair trade: I don't want to be like my grandparents! They were tea growers in Sri Lanka and I don't think they treated their staff very well, but in those days that was the norm. Now, it's a different matter. In many ways, it's a shame that fair trade is something that has to be promoted and campaigned for; it should just happen anyway. Unfortunately, the downside of our current trading system (which no-one is silly enough to promote as 'Unfair Trade', even though it's accurate) needs to be revealed in order for customers to pay attention.

Jeremy movingly describes some of the terrible struggles people face in the Third World, like the children living on the railway stations in India and the girls sold into prostitution in Nepal, and then goes on to show how fair trade can and is benefiting such people. Now, for a homeless person on the streets to become a fashion designer or retail manager – that's real achievement, and it's accomplished by regular folk making small changes. A new morality is growing among consumers. I would love to see the press picking this up and adding to its momentum.

There are not enough good news stories and fair trade really should be covered in much more depth. *Coffins, Cats And Fair Trade Sex Toys* (what a title!) offers the reader a unique insight into the fair trade world to help us all understand what it is truly about: people.

I believe the public understand the concept of fair trade: everyone around the world should be able to send their kids to school, to buy them books, keep them safe and afford to feed them. Fair trade has the public's trust. *Coffins, Cats And Fair Trade Sex Toys* will add to this. It's rare to find a book about a 'serious issue' that is well-written, informative and amusing, but Jeremy's managed it without sermonising. The book is deceptively light-hearted, as Jeremy isn't afraid to poke fun at himself. He remembers his early days of working on the tills in his first store: subconsciously smiling at customers who didn't want a plastic bag, and scowling at those who did. Plastic bags are an important issue for us all, and highlight the current divide between caring for the environment and trying to reduce poverty. I've probably cut my consumption down by 90% by keeping reusable jute bags in my car – that way I usually remember them when I go shopping. Jute bags are improving the environment in the UK: but if they're not fairly traded, then surely they're increasing poverty in the Third World where they're produced?

I've been passionate about organic food for years now and agree with Jeremy that fair trade and the environmental and organic movements have much to learn from one another. We should work closer together. Poverty, over-consumption and global warming are three of the greatest problems we face in the world today: but they are not insurmountable if we all work together to solve them. You can help by reducing your carbon footprint and recycling. But perhaps the simplest way you can change our planet is to buy fair trade products. And as a way of showing you how it works and why you should do it, I can't recommend this book to you enough.

Antony Worrall Thompson

1 A Gift For My Mother?

"CAN YOU TELL me where your fair trade products are, please?" I asked a supermarket assistant a few years ago. She looked blank.

"Have you *heard* of fair trade?" I continued. Her face told all. Obviously not.

Such a response would be unlikely today. Almost everyone in Britain has heard of fair trade. It's a fantastic phenomenon! It used to be associated with benevolent idealists, political activists and ageing hippies, but this is no longer the case. It's now a popular cause and it's supported by people of all ages, opinions and lifestyles.

My mother is one of the many people in Britain who supports fair trade. She buys the odd jar of fair trade coffee, an occasional bar of chocolate for her grandchildren, and sometimes a gift or two when she visits Shared Earth – the fair trade shop that I started in York in 1986. And, of course, she also agrees it's a 'Good Thing.' However, like many people who support fair trade, she doesn't know much about it.

I recently heard of a new and unusual fair trade business in Kent. By chance, it's very close to where my mother lives, near Sevenoaks. An ideal opportunity, I thought, for her to learn more about fair trade. Why not combine my next visit to her with a visit to this new business?

Initially my mother seemed quite keen on the idea of going for a pub lunch with a fair trade friend of mine. But now came the difficult part. How to tell her the nature of this business? This was not just any old fair trade enterprise selling tea, coffee or embroidered scarves. The product

was not the sort of thing you find on a supermarket shelf. Or on the shelves of any high street store. In fact, you wouldn't find it in even the most dedicated fair trade shop. And it's the last thing you'd give your 84-year old mother as a birthday present.

"Yes, I'd be interested in learning more about fair trade," my mother said. "But what does this company sell?"

This was the difficult bit.

"Well, er, actually," I stammered, "well, to tell you the truth – well, actually, he sells, er," I was struggling for words. It was a sensitive subject. "Actually, he sells coffins."

"Oh, I see," replied my mother.

"It's nothing personal," I added. "I mean…" At this point I thought it would be better to say no more.

✶✶✶

We set off late on a sunny day at the end of August. Kent – the 'garden of England' – had never looked lovelier. We looked out for orchards but never saw any; apparently many of them have been cut down, because so much of the fruit the supermarkets sell now comes from cheaper sources abroad. Eventually, after driving down a long track, there was the sign: ECOFFINS. The 'E' and the play on the word 'eco' indicate that it's intended to be an environmentally-friendly business, as well as a fair trade one.

Ecoffins' owner, William Wainman, was there to meet us. He has wavy brown hair, an innocent smile and a weather-beaten face. You can almost imagine him from his name alone, driving a cart along a country lane. The dour expression which one associates with people in his trade was not evident, and we happily strolled to the local pub, and enjoyed an excellent lunch. Then it was back for a tour of the premises.

An intriguing sign caught my eye. "Is that some kind of award?" I asked. I was told that Ecoffins, which was founded in 2000, had won the 'Natural Death Handbook Award' for the Best Coffin Manufacturer in the UK, only four years later. An impressive start. Before Ecoffins, William had run a business in Hunan Province, China, making bamboo furniture. He was then approached by the British Embassy in Beijing.

They were receiving regular enquiries for bamboo coffins – from people in the UK who were concerned about the environment and wanted an alternative to wood.

William was worried. What would the craftsmen, who were used to making furniture, think?

"I told them a customer had ordered some baskets for extremely large fish," he told us. "I thought they would want to down their tools and leave if they knew what they were making. But the secret soon came out. Luckily, they didn't seem to mind when they found out what the 'fish baskets' really were. They seemed very relaxed about it. Though it didn't make any difference," he added, "to the number of cigarettes they were smoking."

From then on, the demand for coffins grew and grew, until it displaced the furniture altogether. Bamboo is an excellent sustainable material. It's quick-growing, only taking two months to reach its full height – a truly renewable resource, whose use in this way reduces the demand for precious hardwoods. Also, in case anyone reading this is worried, apparently the bamboo used by Ecoffins is a different species from the one eaten by giant pandas.

"But isn't it harmful to the environment, shipping them all the way from China?" asked my son, who had accompanied us. A good question, I thought, from someone who was only twelve at the time. But it posed no problem for William, who had obviously been asked it many times before.

"Not at all," he explained, "the different sizes are packed Russian-doll style; and we even fill the space in the smallest coffin with nameplates, headboards and other accessories. Shipping is less harmful than many people think, despite the distance. It's air freight that really does the damage. I've worked out that from a carbon footprint point of view, shipping one coffin to the UK is roughly equivalent to driving a car for just three or four miles."

I was impressed. It's great to see products that are not just environmentally-friendly, but fairly traded too. Ecoffins was the first British company to attain fair trade status in China. And the coffins looked very attractive. I almost felt like asking my mother to climb into one to try it out.

By this time we had made our way outside and were looking around the three old farm buildings which served as warehouses, inside which the coffins were stored, awaiting orders and despatch. The different types and sizes – they can even be made to measure – were stacked against the walls in rows. An excellent photo opportunity, I thought, and my mother obligingly posed.

I could tell she was interested too, by the questions she was asking and the number of leaflets she took away with her. Was she thinking of passing them around amongst her friends? She's not the sort of person who would run a fair trade tea and coffee stall. Perhaps instead she could become the local agent for Ecoffins in her village? She could supplement her income by taking a small commission on each sale. I tried to imagine her as a door-to-door saleswoman, peddling the advantages of fair trade, eco-friendly coffins to her elderly neighbours. She is in the right age group to be convincing…

Death is a subject that we rarely speak about, and many of us shy away from even thinking about it. Sometimes this is because of pain or sadness, but sometimes it's just embarrassment. It's a pity we can't discuss it more openly. Why are we so afraid? When I die, I'd like to be buried in one of William's coffins. It's rewarding to think that even when I'm dead, I'll be doing something positive with my life.

✶✶✶

Most people in this country have now heard of fair trade. It's often linked with the complex problems of the world: globalisation, poverty, inequality, dwindling resources and so on. But it's part of the solution, not the problem. In the last twenty years we, as consumers, have become much more aware of our purchasing power. From the sweatshops where brand-label trainers, sportswear and clothing are made, to the fields where children work long hours and have no chance of going to school, there's a spectrum of exploitation and so-called employment which is often closer to slavery. But reports in the media have brought these issues to our attention. We feel uncomfortable when we see them. They don't fit in with our cherished ideas of justice, fairness and opportunity.

And while we once felt powerless to do anything about it, the message

is finally getting through that we're not; as consumers, we have a great deal of power. We are asking more and more questions. This product that we hold in our hands: where and how was it made? Who made it? Do they get a fair wage? Were children involved? Is it contributing to global warming? And so on.

We have realised that by buying – or not buying – a product, we can help to make small changes in what seems like a smaller and more fragile world.

Even politicians are finding fair trade useful to promote their image. For MPs, it's almost as good as kissing babies or cycling to the House of Commons. "For the first time ever, international development has been an election issue," said a senior civil servant after the Make Poverty History campaign in 2005. Along with carbon footprinting, fair trade is one of the most buzzworthy topics around.

And how could it not be? In the last fifty years, the conditions of everyday life for hundreds of millions in the developing world have worsened. There seem to be more disasters each year, and we see heart-wrenching images on television of children dying from starvation, refugees fleeing from war and families flooded out of their homes. In addition, there are countless good causes to support at home – medical research, care for the elderly, homelessness... the list goes on and on. And then there are the beggars we see in our streets. It seems as if we're being asked for donations all the time. How much can we do? We can't support everyone. Yet most of us really want to help.

Fair trade has become a magical answer. You don't have to make donations. By buying fair trade products, you can do as much good as charities, helping the people who really need it. In fact, you can do more, because if trade becomes fairer, and people throughout the world can make a better living for themselves, there wouldn't be the need for some of these charities in the first place. Whilst natural disasters will always happen, poorer countries will be better able to cope for themselves, making overseas aid less important.

So, the reasoning goes, buy fair trade and you'll help to create a better world. You don't have to make donations; all you have to do is choose the right brands when you do your shopping.

Yet if it's really that simple, why isn't the world already a better place?

Whilst market forces are complex, the answer lies largely in the way big business works, and its need for ever greater profits. Corporations are accountable to their shareholders, no matter what the cost to people or planet. Trade terms are stacked in favour of the rich nations, and large corporations have enormous power, both to influence the media and to affect government policy. They can also damage local economies by moving factories to – or buying goods from – another country.

They can gain influence in poorer countries by methods which would be illegal in Britain or Europe – providing perks to politicians who vote sympathetically, for instance. In countries where corruption is rife, politicians often earn more in this way than they do from their normal work. A bribe here, the funding of a government project there – and a lot of blind eyes can be turned to a company's more dubious activities.

To be fair, of course, all businesses provide jobs, and successful businesses can improve our local economy and living standards, in both the developed and the developing world. And if that success has been achieved by paying low wages, using child labour, or polluting the environment? Well, a lot of us don't want to know. It's on the other side of the world, and anyway, isn't the company which makes the goods responsible, not us?

That's why fair trade is such an important change of direction. It's making us think about these things, and take responsibility for them ourselves, as individuals who can choose what we buy. Everyone is against child labour, and no-one wants to destroy the planet. None of us likes the idea of people working for fifteen hours a day and still not earning enough to feed their families. But until recently most of us have felt too busy, powerless or apathetic to do anything about it. Most of us have become resigned to the way the system works and just accept it.

With fair trade, this is changing. People are realising they *can* affect what happens in the world. One person buying a jar of fair trade coffee doesn't change anything: but when a million people buy fair trade coffee, it has a real impact on the lives of the coffee producers. This is what's happening – more and more people are choosing to buy fair trade. In our own small way, each one of us is helping the people abroad who are making those goods.

As the number of people buying fair trade grows, so does our power

as consumers. We are starting to have an influence on the politicians who can change the laws, and an influence on big business, which will respond to market forces and change its practices.

Politicians are seeing how many people support fair trade, and are starting to realise that unjust trading regulations need to be addressed. Some, as individuals, would like things to change anyway. Now, as they see that this would be popular with their electorate, there are signs that it may be starting to affect party policy.

Supermarkets are being faced with a stark choice. Should they go on selling products they've bought at the cheapest possible prices in order to make more profit? Or should they take into account the lives of producers and the well-being of the environment? The boards of some very large supermarkets are beginning to realise that it's the latter course that will win the hearts – and therefore the wallets – of their customers. As a result, more and more fair trade products are appearing on their shelves.

There are similarities between the fair trade movement and some campaigns that took place in the nineteenth and early twentieth centuries, like the fight for better working conditions in factories and the movement to abolish child labour. In many respects, fair trade is campaigning for similar things, but its target is the global marketplace in which we all now live. This makes significant change more difficult to achieve and campaigning can be a slow, even fruitless process. Fair trade is, in contrast, a form of direct action – your money goes where you want it to go. It's that simple.

A lot of progress is being made. Chain stores are commissioning reports to ensure that the products they buy are not made by children. Some are starting to monitor suppliers to ensure that reasonable wages are being paid, that health and safety regulations are enforced and that working hours do not go beyond legal limits. Others are taking steps to promote sustainable production, reduce carbon emissions and recycle waste. Some are replacing hardwoods with wood from trees which grow to maturity more quickly. More and more products with the Fairtrade Mark are appearing, both on supermarket shelves and in the high street.

How exciting that we, as consumers, are making this happen!

2 The Birth Of Fair Trade

FAIR TRADE IS available on the high street and the internet, on trains, in gift shops, corner shops, cafes, museums, art galleries – even zoos and funeral parlours! It's become a mass movement. How did it all start?

To find the answer, you have to look at how our attitudes have changed over the last fifty years. I come from a generation whose parents went through the Second World War, and their values and aspirations were defined by it. They fought in every corner of the globe, or if they stayed at home, they saved to cope with rationing, dug for victory and donated their saucepans to help the war effort. Many of them suffered from bombing raids, and children were taken from their parents and evacuated to the countryside. Their future was unknown and uncertain. Relatives and friends were killed, disabled or taken prisoner: whole families and communities were disrupted or destroyed.

When the war ended, they wanted two things above all else: security and prosperity. They were tired of scrimping and saving and they wanted their children to have a safe and trouble-free future. The only change they wanted was to move away from uncertainty and into material prosperity. In the 1950s, many of them got what they wanted. Things did become more secure in Britain, and the standard of living did improve – at least in Europe, America and the other developed nations.

But those of us who grew up after the war were not as appreciative as we might have been. The security which our parents craved was dull and limited for us. Weren't there better aims in life than finding a well-paid

job, buying a new television, starting a family and having two children? We questioned everything. Wasn't there more to life than money? Why should women just stay at home and have children? Was the food we ate healthy? Could we learn from other religions? What was wrong with being gay? Was it right that we were so well-off, while so many in the 'Third World' were poor?

Growing your hair long, wearing unconventional clothes and listening to rock music were expressions of our discontent. Some of us 'dropped out' to explore different ways of living and working. We blamed 'the establishment' for the apparent failure of society to solve the world's problems; the normal political channels – becoming a councillor or an MP and trying to change the laws – just didn't seem to be worthwhile. It wasn't just laws anyway – we wanted to change people's attitudes to life. We talked about an 'alternative society'; new expressions like 'alternative medicine', 'alternative technology' and 'alternative religions' came into vogue. It seemed like the whole world was bursting with new ideas.

Some of us were engaged in political protest, others in the arts or media, others in education or community work. Often we got it wrong. Yet underneath was a sincere idealism. How could we make the world a better place to live in?

There wasn't a facet of society that wasn't touched. We questioned everything, even business. In fact, business was key to the change that was to take place in the years ahead. Previously, if you cared about justice or the gap between rich and poor, you looked for solutions in economic and political systems. To make change, you changed the government. Maybe you even wanted to throw out capitalism and replace it with communism.

In the 1960s and 70s this started to change. Young people were disillusioned with politics. Some of us were just bored; politicians all seemed the same. We gave up hope on things changing from the top down. We started trying to change our own lives, and from them the communities around us – and eventually, we hoped, the whole world.

Instead of trying to change the government, some of us opened shops. Traditional shops and supermarkets often didn't have what we wanted, so we opened wholefood shops, 'alternative' bookshops and health clinics. We started organic farms, community printshops, even schools. There

was a ready market for these new businesses and they flourished. It was the start of the 'ethical' shopping movement which is so widespread today.

'Alternative trade' was a part of this movement. It referred specifically to trade with developing nations. It was only later, in the second half of the 1980s, that the term 'fair trade' replaced it. It was a new concept and exactly what it meant was still unclear. It was often thought of as a way of missing out the middlemen and buying direct, to ensure that producers received a better share of the profits and weren't exploited.

We knew that conventional trading relationships between developed and developing countries were unfair and unjust. The growth of trade after the war had brought great benefits, but the aim of trade was to maximise profit and the wealthier nations had the power to ensure that the terms of trade were in their favour. As global trade grew, the model of free market economics became a mockery.

In the 1950s and 60s, the former colonies of Asia, Africa and Latin America were encouraged to export, in the hope that this would benefit their economies and thus the world economy generally. In some countries – notably in Japan and the 'tiger' economies of South East Asia – it worked. In most, especially in Africa, it was a dismal failure. The poorer countries became stuck in a trap. They ended up producing food and raw materials, which are notoriously subject to price fluctuation. The profits from manufacturing, packaging and distribution went abroad. Even if they wanted to export manufactured goods, the poor countries found it very hard to compete.

Multinational companies grew to wield enormous power. They received subsidies from governments, whether in the form of tax breaks, handouts and access to free scientific research, or in the form of infrastructure – roads, airports and so on. They were also assisted by tariff barriers. Governments were worried about unemployment; companies by loss of profit. So tariffs – usually taxes on manufactured goods – were introduced to protect key industries. Quotas on the amount that the developing countries could export fulfilled a similar function.

As world trade grew, some multinationals became larger than national governments. Small states in Africa and the Caribbean were encouraged to grow single crops, like coffee or bananas, and then became reliant

on them for income. Sometimes, the multinationals left communities in ruins as they swapped suppliers and countries. Subsidies to farmers in the developed countries made things even worse, allowing some producers to export at below the cost of production. This undercut farmers in developing countries. Prices went down on the world market.

The multinationals were guided by profit, not human lives; they bought from whoever gave the lowest price. Suppliers usually had no choice; a little money was better than none at all. They reduced prices to stop buyers going elsewhere. Prices went down in our supermarkets; our standard of living went up. Poverty went up in the third world; their standard of living went down. The poor became poorer, the rich richer.

Inside the poorer nations, small-scale producers were often exploited by middlemen and money-lenders. The agents of large companies bribed local officials to ignore labour laws and environmental regulations. Child labour increased. Although factory conditions became abysmal, with long working hours and appalling wages, we in the West remained ignorant. We just saw cheaper prices in our shops, and a growing selection of goods to choose from. Our standard of living was rising, and we were happy.

Fair trade was a response to all of this. The awareness that people were suffering prompted some of us to action, especially those in the Church. Others had a more political agenda and were concerned about the increasing injustice of world trade.

Activists in the poorer nations were also concerned. Some had been campaigning against exploitation long before the Second World War. Mahatma Gandhi, the champion of the untouchables, was one; his crusades to improve the lot of the 'poorest of the poor' mirror the aims of the fair trade movement today. Mahaguthi, a well-known fair trade producer group in Nepal today, was founded in 1924 by Tulsi Mehar Shrestha (the 'Gandhi of Nepal.') Like Gandhi, he promoted community development and trained people in the production of Khadi (hand-spun) cloth.

These initiatives aimed to promote self-reliance and emphasised local trade – if trade was involved at all. Today's fair trade movement grew up as a response to a world in which trade is increasingly global in nature. Most fair trade today is about the relationships between buyers

in Europe, North America and other developed countries and producers in Africa, Asia and Latin America.

Fair trade shops have been around for longer than most people realise. In the 1940s, two American organisations, the Mennonite Central Committee and SERRV International, started buying from poor communities and sold their handicrafts, such as needlework and jute baskets, in churches and charity stores. The first shop selling these and other items opened in the USA in 1958.

The current fair trade movement took off in Europe in the 1960s. Oxfam, founded in 1942 to help hungry civilians in occupied Greece, opened its first shop in 1948, below its offices in Oxford. Initially, it sold donated second-hand goods, but in the late 1950s it started to sell crafts made by Chinese refugees. Further shops followed in Guildford, Leeds and Cheltenham, and not long after, in the mid-sixties, Oxfam launched its 'Helping by Selling' programme. Handicrafts were imported and sold through its shops and a mail order catalogue, providing employment for people at the bottom of society, increasing their opportunities and improving their lives.

It's hard to imagine what a big step forward this was at the time. Previously, Oxfam had bought crafts from commercial importers to raise funds for its aid work. Where and how they were made was not considered important. "When I visited one of these importers," recalled Roy Scott, who was the inspiration behind the new scheme, "he congratulated Oxfam's astute buying, because much income for Oxfam's work could be made by buying cheap and selling at a good profit. I had to persuade the charity's trading board that what it was doing could be considered exploitation."

Meanwhile, in the Netherlands, Dutch third world groups were selling cane sugar with the message that 'by buying cane sugar you give people in poor countries a place in the sun of prosperity.' The importer Fair Trade Organisatie was set up in 1967 and in 1969 the first European 'World Shop' opened in Utrecht. Dozens more were soon trading, mostly in the Benelux countries and Germany. All were run by dedicated volunteers.

For many, fair trade in the 1970s was a political response to 'neo-colonialism.' Most of the former colonies had achieved independence by then, but political independence was not the same as economic independence. Many small nations relied on cash crops. Their income came from global corporations which were owned by their former colonial masters.

Radical student movements started attacking these multinational corporations and the power they held over people's lives. The Nestlé boycott was launched in 1977 as a response to Nestlé's marketing tactics in developing countries. Free samples of baby milk powder were being given to young mothers. While they fed their babies with milk powder, their own breast milk dried up. They were then forced to buy the infant formula, which they could not afford. Even today, millions of children die because their mothers don't breastfeed. Poor mothers over-dilute baby milk powder with water to make it last longer, which can cause malnutrition, and the water itself may be contaminated. Diarrhoea is a big killer in developing countries.

McDonald's also came under attack. To satisfy the demand for burgers, huge swathes of Amazon rainforest were being destroyed to provide grazing land for cattle. The rainforest is still being felled today. Cattle farming to produce beef is still widespread, and the rainforest is also increasingly threatened by commodity crops like soya and biofuels. The fertility of the soil deteriorates quickly, and the land becomes unproductive. More trees then have to be cut down, leading to a vicious spiral of destruction.

Some people in the 1970s questioned the very basis of 'capitalist society.' The model of free market economics was coming under intense scrutiny – it might be great for some, but was it all it was made out to be? It was already apparent what a struggle it was for the poor in the developing world to feed their families. Fair trade activists were starting to realise how quotas and trading regulations were stacked in favour of the rich nations – and how, for many at the bottom of society, it was impossible to step up the ladder at all. Activists started selling coffee from Angola and Nicaragua at stalls in churches, colleges and on the street. The Anti-Apartheid Movement blossomed; 'solidarity' became the new in-word, and the slogan 'Trade not Aid' gained increasing recognition.

People with humanitarian motives – often members of the Church – found they had common ground with left-wingers who were concerned about justice. Many right-wing economists who believed in self-help supported fair trade too, as Richard Adams notes in his book *Who Profits?*. They commend it "for enabling people to stand on their own feet and become self-reliant and not depend on hand-outs."

But it wasn't easy. The 'politicals' weren't too keen on the Christians. They disliked them for their conservativism. And the Christians and conservatives were suspicious of the 'politicals', who were too radical for their liking.

The aim of Oxfam's 'Helping by Selling' programme had been to raise funds for Oxfam's aid work. If it reduced unemployment at the same time, that was an added bonus, but that wasn't the purpose. Fair wages, good working conditions, continuity of orders and other standard fair trade issues were not yet a priority.

Roy Scott now proposed a new kind of trading in which the underlying theme would be long-term partnership. The aim would be to benefit not Oxfam, but the producers. Profits from sales would go back to them, to develop their businesses and communities. This was a radical proposal at the time, but it was eventually accepted in 1975 under the name Bridge. Within 15 years, nearly 300 groups of producers in 43 countries were involved, and annual turnover was £8 million. Left wing politics and Christian caring were coming together and making an impact.

There was one issue on which the 'politicals' and the Christians agreed completely, however. They all thought fair trade coffee tasted awful.

"That horrendous coffee from Tanzania did the movement a lot of harm," commented Ruth Minich, who managed a fair trade shop in Leeds at the time. "It was more like medicine." It reminded some older people of chicory or the 'ersatz' coffee made from acorns or barley which they had drunk in the war.

Things have changed today – fair trade coffee competes with the best. But in the seventies, as one wit remarked, "Only vicars would be mad enough to buy it."

Apart from the early Oxfam shops, probably the first fair trade shop in the UK was opened in London in 1973 by Benny Dembitzer under the name Project Hand. Having spent a year in Africa visiting a number of development projects, he came to realise that none of them – however much they funded education, health or social welfare – allowed people to stand on their own two feet by developing their own businesses. Project Hand was an attempt to enable artisans to move beyond their limited local markets and sell their crafts in the high street abroad. Unfortunately, the timing was wrong. The UK economy was in ruins in 1973; and to make matters worse, an Oxfam shop opened nearby, reducing Project Hand's sales. It closed in 1975.

Meanwhile, Richard Adams, a theological college drop-out, was also making his mark on the fair trade scene in London. What was the Church doing, he asked, to bring justice into a world where so many suffered needlessly? He learned how peasants in rural India were only earning 1p a kilo for crops like French beans, which later sold for 70p a kilo in London's Covent Garden market. Disappointed by the Church's lack of action, he decided to take the initiative himself and opened a greengrocer's shop.

Nowadays there aren't many greengrocers around – the supermarkets have seen to that. This one started in a particularly unusual way, with a visit to India, and a Gandhian-style walk from village to village to survey the type of crops grown by small farmers. Soon, with a couple of college friends, Richard was running a shop in Sudbury Hill, London. It sold not just potatoes, onions and greens, but exotic fruits and vegetables from around the world. The aim was to cut out the middlemen and get more of the profits back to the farmers who grew the crops.

In 1974 Richard was approached by a Baptist missionary on behalf of The Jute Works, a co-operative in Bangladesh which made baskets, bags, mats and sikas (hanging baskets for indoor plant-pots) from local jute. The aftermath of the war against Pakistan had left thousands of women widowed and a cyclone and flooding had made their situation worse. They desperately needed some means to earn a living. Crafts offered real possibilities. The materials were sustainable and cheap, and the work involved traditional skills. But the local market was saturated. Could Richard help?

He had no idea how he was going to sell them, especially in a greengrocer's shop, but he agreed, and placed an order. A leaflet listing eleven items was sent out to a couple of hundred friends and contacts. The jute was a massive success, especially the sikas. Richard had hit the jackpot. Perhaps unwittingly, he was importing just what consumers were looking for.

He joined forces with a recently established charity, TEAR Fund, which was set up after an appeal for disaster relief in 1968. TEAR Fund was chartering a plane to send blankets and medical supplies to Bangladesh. As the plane would be coming back empty, they asked Richard if he would like to go out ahead of the flight and buy handicrafts to fill it.

"Who is going to pay for them?" Richard asked. TEAR Fund's response was a surprise. They asked him how much a plane-load of crafts would cost. He made a wild guess, "£10,000?" A cheque for this amount arrived through the post a few days later – and he was off.

He only had ten days, and finding enough crafts was a struggle. It was not a question of ordering 500 of this design and 1,000 of that. He had to take anything that was available, in any quantity, seconds and all. The artisans at The Jute Works were delighted. Eventually, he was scouring street stalls around Dhaka in a lorry, buying up bamboo and cane furniture to fill the plane.

The problem of how to sell it still remained. TEAR Fund hadn't told him how, and selling £10,000 worth of jute through a greengrocer's shop was going to be difficult. Well, he thought, it's a long flight back: there's plenty of time to work that out.

Some time previously, a friend in Northumberland had suggested that Richard should set up a mail order business on Tyneside to sell his jute. Rents were cheaper there, and for the same wages you could obtain a higher standard of living than in London. Richard proposed the idea to TEAR Fund, who accepted it. Soon the boxes of jute and cane were travelling up the A1 motorway to their new home: below the floorboards of a school gym in Newcastle.

The greengrocer's shop closed down and the name Tearcraft was registered. Its first catalogue went out to TEAR Fund's 7,000 supporters in February, 1975. The response was immediate and enthusiastic; as Richard put it, "the local sub post office experienced a spectacular

increase in its parcel traffic and sales of stamps." TEAR Fund supporters were soon joined by shops, which wanted to buy the jute and cane in bulk. This increased orders, and work for the producers, even more. Richard was keen to promote this commercial trade because he didn't want fair trade to become just the concern of a minority church clique.

A new way of contributing to global development emerged. Previously you gave money or second-hand goods to a charity, and let them get on with it. Now you could be involved directly yourself. You could buy fair trade products. You could help even more by selling them too. Soon hundreds of 'voluntary representatives' (or 'reps') were involved, as Richard describes in *Who Profits?*:

"Organisations for the young and old signed up; people used the products for all types of causes from raising funds for their church hall to supporting reconstruction in Hanoi. Tearcraft had been able to provide a new, practical method of Third World support that people could adopt in their own way."

In its first three years Tearcraft grew rapidly. By 1978 it had over thirty staff, a huge warehouse, suppliers in ten countries, and sales of over half a million pounds.

Tensions, however, were emerging. TEAR Fund – an evangelical Christian organisation – wanted Tearcraft to purchase its crafts solely from groups organised by, or associated with, evangelical Christians. For Richard and most of his staff, this would lead "to the suspicion that TEAR Fund is more concerned about its supporters than about those it supports." They opposed it. The different viewpoints could not be reconciled and a parting of the ways became inevitable.

An agreement was reached. Richard was allowed to buy the stock from the producers who were not specifically evangelical Christians. This amounted to over a hundred lines and these formed the basis of the first catalogue from Richard's new venture, which became known as Traidcraft. The name was taken from the name of a shop in Bristol run by local Tearcraft reps. It had opened as a concession inside another store in 1977 but, despite a heady start with Cliff Richard present, it soon closed. It was now possible for Tearcraft to buy the ready-formed company, transfer its shares and use its name.

Today's Traidcraft, the largest fair trade organisation in the UK, has

its origins in retail – a greengrocer's shop in London, and a handicraft shop in Bristol. Traidcraft's first catalogue went out in 1979, and within days the orders were pouring in. In its first year, with sales of £123,000, a respectable profit of £12,000 was made. Traidcraft has never looked back. Its turnover today is £23 million.

Traidcraft's voluntary reps were (and are) essential to its success. Committed and motivated, they are excellent at talking to people about where the products are from and why fair trade is so special. Their enthusiasm is infectious. In the 1980s and 90s, they helped to spread the word in schools, churches, trade unions – anywhere, in fact, that gave them the opportunity to set up their table, display their products and talk about fair trade.

Fair trade is a movement which grew from the grass roots up. From the start, a constant theme of most talks about fair trade was that every purchase and every customer counts. Traidcraft reps and other fair trade campaigners were insistent on this point. "Whenever you go to a supermarket," they said, "ask – again and again – whether they stock fair trade tea, or coffee, or sugar. Ask to see the manager; write to their head office – get the point across!"

The supermarkets started to realise that these were not isolated requests from a few eccentrics. They could, perhaps, represent a new consumer trend. Finally, in 1994, Sainsbury's placed its first order for Fairtrade chocolate – and from there things really took off.

Before that happened, however, a lot of groundwork needed to be done. As Traidcraft, Oxfam and Tearcraft grew, and new fair trade products became available, it wasn't long before shops started opening to sell them. For anyone concerned about development, they were an exciting new concept. They weren't just campaigning and they weren't just raising funds. They were doing both. It wasn't just charity, either. It was trade – fair trade. Producers were earning their living and gaining self-respect. They were trading, not asking for hand-outs.

The first shops were not set up with the aim of making a profit. The people who ran them – often Traidcraft or Tearcraft reps – were usually inexperienced in business and relied on customer goodwill rather than good products, merchandising and customer care. They were often perceived as 'do-gooders.' In business circles, they were not seen as a serious retail venture.

"People called us the beard and sandals brigade," recalled Ruth Minich, whose shop in Leeds was owned by Traidcraft. "Fair trade was seen as a mad scheme that hippies had come up with, and it was difficult to prove ourselves because we were immediately labelled."

Shops opened wherever there were people enthusiastic enough to start them. Possibly the first successful fair trade shop in Britain was the Coach House in Balmore, Scotland. It was (and still is) in one of the most obscure locations imaginable, in the middle of the countryside about seven miles from Glasgow. An outbuilding in the garden of a large house, it had been a coffee shop, but closed down in 1972 when John and Nena Riches bought the property and turned it into their office.

In 1979 they visited South Africa and returned eager to raise money for development projects there. The outhouse in their garden seemed ideal and, with a group of friends, they converted it into a shop selling crafts, mostly from Oxfam, which opened in May 1980. Three years later, they were visited by Angela Gomez, who was working with women on the streets in Bangladesh.

"Most of these women," explained John, "had lost their husbands, and many had been raped during the War of Independence. Now they were outcasts, surviving on wages of about $1 a month from menial jobs, if they could find work at all. Angela was organising them into small groups and starting to find work for them with a new handicraft project called Kumdini."

John and Nena, moved by the plight of these women, offered Angela a grant from the Balmore Trust, which distributes the profits from their shop. The reply was unexpected.

"I don't want your money!" she said. "But I do want you to sell the women's handicrafts. It will give them a wage, and just as important, it will give them back their dignity."

From then on, the concept of fair trade, as opposed to simply fund-raising for development projects, became increasingly important for John and Nena. The Coach House, along with Project Hand, was one of the first fair trade businesses to import crafts from Africa – "before people thought you could even have crafts from Africa," as John put it. It rented halls in Glasgow to exhibit paintings and baskets from Namibia, soapstone from Kenya, woven carpets from Ethiopia and

wonderful Zulu jewellery – at the same time promoting the ideas of fair trade to anyone who was interested. The most successful exhibition was of 25 beautiful quilts from Soweto, which arrived just after the Soweto uprising. They sold for about £300 each (the equivalent of over £1,000 today) and fifteen of them sold immediately.

The Coach House was on a minor road in the countryside, but with a manager like Jan Brown – who "was so keen she would hardly let anyone out of the door until they'd bought something" – sales flourished, and the shop is still open today.

Other early fair trade shops in the UK included Juteronomy in Kenilworth, World of Difference in Rugby and Justicia in Bolton. The main problem at this time was the lack of available stock. Apart from Oxfam, Tearcraft and Traidcraft, not much was available, and none of them gave wholesale discounts which would enable their trade customers to make a decent margin. This made paying commercial rents difficult. Almost all fair trade shops at this time opened in back streets or other out-of-the-way locations, restricting sales and their ability to promote the fair trade message.

Traidcraft, however, with mail order and rep sales booming, teamed up with Christian Aid under the name Tradefair to open a chain of stores. Advertisements were placed for a Retail Manager and the successful candidate, Mark Patchett, was appointed in 1984. "I was extremely surprised to get the job," he said. "I had been selling scaffolding and my knowledge of retail was pretty well zero. All I had was a lot of enthusiasm. But that was typical of everyone in fair trade at that time – we had lots of energy and we were excited about the opportunities. Hardly any of us had any real practical experience."

Traidcraft already had a shop in Newcastle and they chose Leicester as a pilot project for the new chain. A professional manager, Wendy Wood, was recruited.

"There's no way I can run a shop with this product range," she said, "and we can't just use the shop to sell through Traidcraft's dead stock." So Traidcraft's buyers visited other fair trade organisations on the continent and placed orders with them to widen the range. The Leicester shop opened in October 1985.

One of the worst teething problems it had was shoplifting. Several

expensive carpets just disappeared, causing considerable anxiety. Then, to promote the shop, an exhibition was set up in the foyer of the local cinema, where *A Passage To India* was showing. It included Traidcraft's pride and joy, some large embroidered elephants which retailed at over £100 each.

"The customers weren't interested in the exhibition," said Mark Patchett. "They just walked off with the elephants without paying for them. The cinema staff didn't notice – and probably didn't care."

The new shop made a loss. Two more were opened, however, in Leeds and Liverpool. Traidcraft's Newcastle shop was performing well, but it was away from the main shopping area, and only fair trade supporters visited it, although their enthusiasm for the cause did not necessarily make them good customers. As Ruth Minich pointed out, "the trouble with our hardcore fair trade customers is that they're not materialistic enough. They love what we're doing, but they don't buy anything."

One very successful venture was the One World Shop in Edinburgh. In October 1982, George Shand started a fair trade stall in a room in the disused basement of a church on Princes Street. George, a minister in the Church of Scotland, had recently divorced; the Church disapproved, and he was forced to seek employment elsewhere. Fair trade was the beneficiary. Initially, the new shop was for the Christmas period only, but George wanted to stay on. Soon he was raising funds to redevelop the whole of the basement. A new, larger shop opened in 1986, and it also took over the adjacent café, which was being run by the Church and was in difficulties.

George decided to take three years off to develop the project. He was as excited as everyone else at that time about the opportunities ahead for fair trade.

"You'd look at the shop and think, my God, we've got so few resources," he remembers. "But there was a fantastic groundswell of people concerned about the impact of their purchasing on others – they wanted to express their values in the way they bought things. The support for the shop from such people was overwhelming."

The Edinburgh Festival was a unique opportunity to promote fair trade, and like the Coach House in Glasgow, the One World Shop started importing crafts and organising exhibitions to coincide with it. Talks were

given to anyone who would invite them. George remembers giving a talk to a group of gruff local miners. Initially, they were extremely sceptical, but when they heard about the problems of the soapstone miners and carvers in Agra, India, they began to relate to these problems and to compare them with those they were facing in their own communities.

"We had a table full of products for sale," says George. "But at the end of the evening, there was nothing left at all. They bought every single piece."

'Commercial' fair trade shops were unusual in the 1980s. Almost all fair trade shops relied on volunteers; most still do. An exception was Tumi, set up by Mo Fini in 1978. He was passionate about South America and was possibly the first person to start importing a wide variety of its crafts into the UK. After meeting Richard Adams in his greengrocer days, Mo became an advisor both to Traidcraft and Oxfam, and supplied Traidcraft for most of the 1980s. Tumi became the UK's best-known wholesaler of South American crafts.

In 1978 ethnic crafts were not easily available. Tumi's evil-looking masks, huge drums, fantastic alpaca jumpers and unusual silver jewellery caught the eye of the public, and they responded eagerly. Mo's first venture was a stall in a craft market in Plymouth, but it was his shops in London and Bath, which opened in 1979 and 1980, which really got Tumi going. Further shops followed in Bristol, Oxford and Brighton.

From the start, Mo earned a living from the business and paid all his staff. His shops were run in a professional manner with lots of attention to display and customer care. Tumi was unusual in other ways, too. Mo's background was different from most fair traders; he was an Iranian immigrant who had no connection with the church. Nor was he particularly interested in politics. He just happened to have travelled to South America and fallen in love with it.

He loved to tell the story of the artisans, and on the walls of Tumi's shops hung pictures illustrating their lives – women from Bolivia wearing their traditional bowler hats, for instance, and children from Peru playing pan-pipes with llamas and mountains in the background.

However, Tumi didn't encourage its customers to buy with stories of poverty, unfair trading terms and the like. It relied on excellent products to achieve its sales. The aim was not to promote the fair trade message; it was simply to do it – to trade fairly, and by doing so to benefit the artisans and their communities.

This set Tumi apart from the 'mainstream' fair trade movement, and Mo never joined any of the organisations which were set up to cater for fair trade importers or retailers. Maybe he had other things on his mind – like survival. The distinctive nature of South American crafts made them liable to swings in fashion, and once they had been around for a few years, customers were looking for something new.

Competition from other countries grew. In the early nineties African crafts became popular, and then Bali, with its fantastic variety of styles, became a focus of attention. Masks, drums and carvings abounded from every continent. More recently China entered the scene, copying everything from everywhere. Machine-made replicas of hand-carved parrots, made from balsa wood in the forests of the Amazon, could now be bought from China. They were nothing like as attractive, but the price was far cheaper. Mo saw this trend with his own eyes when he visited a trade show in Frankfurt in 1992 – the year Tumi's sales peaked.

"It really pissed me off. Peruvian and Mexican jewellery was a large part of our sales at the time, and it was being copied and mass-produced in China. When you're selling a handmade product at $6, and you see a machine-made version of it at $6 a dozen, what can you do? We just couldn't compete."

Tumi struggled with falling sales, and its shops started closing in the second half of the nineties. Today, it only sells online.

When I opened Shared Earth in 1986, there weren't many fair trade shops around. Commercial or non-commercial – as far as I was concerned, they were all doing a good job. I was keen to promote the message, and I was also keen to promote awareness about the environment. But like Mo, I wanted to make a living for myself too. Right from the start, I wanted Shared Earth to be a successful business. But how did I even get involved in the strange world of fair trade? It all began on the hippy trail…

3 The Hippy Trail

LYNNE DAWSON IS one of the stalwarts of fair trade, having worked in it for ten years. When she joined Shared Earth in 1999 it was all completely new to her; now, she is totally committed to it. Lynne is from Manchester and left school at the age of fifteen to become a ballet dancer. In her mid-twenties she went into retail, working in the jewellery and bridal-ware industry, but after twenty years she decided she'd had enough. Shared Earth was just round the corner, and Lynne loved the colours and the textures of our products. One lunch break in 1999, she saw an advert for the job of Manager in our Manchester shop window. She applied, and was accepted.

She was fascinated and quickly threw herself into her work.

"I've known plenty of bosses who say one thing and do another," she said. "But I can see that fair trade isn't just a business principle. You seem to be really committed to it. How did you get involved in the first place?"

It's a question that I'm asked a lot, and I find it hard to answer in a few words. It's been a long journey, and it started off with one particular journey – to India in 1972. The hospitality of the poorest of people, on that first trip to India, will be in my mind forever.

I left school, aged seventeen, in December, 1971. My experience of travelling abroad was limited: a day trip to Calais, a couple of holidays in Austria, and a short school trip to the USSR. The 'Third World' was scary. It brought images to mind of starving African children, Indians hunting with blowpipes, and politicians in native dress, haranguing

crowds in the tropical sun. As a boy I was fascinated by stories of the 'mysterious East', which conjured up more romantic images of Indian snake-charmers, Chinese junks and peasants planting rice. I even used to boast to my friends that I was 'part Chinese', on the basis that my father was born in Shanghai in the 1920s. I thought this somewhat spurious family connection sounded glamorous and alluring. Life in the East seemed a wonderful contrast to the rules and regulations of school, and the certainties of the middle-class suburbia in which I had grown up. It was like Harry Potter and Lawrence of Arabia rolled into one, a dream or fantasy which was as fascinating as it was unattainable.

I was an idealistic teenager, and I yearned to turn the dream into reality. I wanted to escape my humdrum past and travel East. But how to get there? On a camel, winding through the deserts and mountains, perhaps? On the roof of a series of trains, hanging on to the sides if I had to? One thing was certain – travelling by plane did not appeal. It was too expensive, anyway. I decided to hitch-hike overland. Across Europe, then through Turkey, Iran, Afghanistan, Pakistan, and finally to India. The very thought of it was unbelievably exciting to a teenager eager to break the chains of childhood and explore the world. I had never hitch-hiked before, not even in Britain.

After three months of labouring on a building site to earn some money, I was ready to go. My parents, with some apprehension, agreed to drive me to the nearest motorway. This was a relief, because for some reason, I was more worried about how to get from home to a suitable motorway than I was about how to hitch-hike across Europe. We came to a suitable spot. My mother was concerned about the contents of my rucksack; I was travelling light, which I had interpreted as a spare pair of socks, pants and shirt, and a book on survival. I also had a camera, a sleeping bag and a piece of plastic (to sleep on), some string, a water bottle, a knife, fork and plate, a few medicines, an umbrella (which was soon discarded) and, for some reason, a small British flag. I was travelling six thousand miles; she thought I needed more.

It was cold and my heart was beating furiously as I put my thumb up for the first time. My parents had left and I was on my own. Would people stop? How long would I have to wait? The start of that journey was one of the most anxious moments of my life.

Someone soon slowed down and stopped a few yards along the motorway. This didn't ease the tension; I remember my heart beating even faster. I gathered my rucksack and ran to open the door, afraid the driver would change their mind and drive on before I got there. I was even more afraid of being a passenger in someone else's car – a complete stranger about whom I knew nothing. I wasn't frightened of being attacked or molested – I don't think that even crossed my mind. I was nervous for a different reason, which seems comical now. How do you make conversation, I wondered, with someone you've never met before and whose life is completely different from your own?

I need not have worried. It was easier than I thought: the driver who picked me up did all the talking. Soon I was approaching Dover, and my first big hurdle – the English Channel. As a boy I had been imprisoned at boarding school for many years. My favourite kind of reading was prisoner-of-war escape stories like *The Wooden Horse* and *The Colditz Story*. They gave me the romantic notion that I might cross the Channel by stowing away in a ship.

Reality proved different. After a quick look around Dover, I wondered how they could possibly have got away with it. Despite a few misgivings about compromising my ideals so early on in my journey, I paid my fare across the Channel.

Soon I was travelling across the broad German autobahns, and then through the communist countries of Eastern Europe: Hungary, Romania and Bulgaria. Gradually the cars became fewer, the roads and signs less well-kept, and the economies more agricultural. Horses and carts started appearing. The standardised houses and work-clothes of the communist regime of Hungary gave way to the quainter buildings of Romania, and then Bulgaria. I saw animals in the streets, women in black shawls and men with ferocious-looking beards. In Bulgaria I had competition – people of all ages, from young children to old women, stood alongside me trying to get lifts. There weren't many vehicles on the road, and most were full. I was on the border of Europe, each mile a further step into unknown territory.

Right on the border of East and West stood the bustling city of Istanbul with its mixture of old and new. Modern offices soared up beside relics of the Ottoman and Byzantine empires. Clean-shaven men in suits and ties

walked along the pavements beside men with skull-caps and colourful waistcoats; women in the latest fashions vied with others in dark dresses and shawls to buy food in the busy market-places. A cacophony of voices, hooting cars and animals barking or bleating seemed to greet you wherever you went. The sound of strange music drifted out of cafés on to the streets; mullahs called the faithful to prayer.

Istanbul was a meeting place for travellers from around the world. I was staying in the cheapest hotels possible, the next step up from sleeping rough. You shared a room with several others, toilets were a hole in the floor, and the nightly charge was about 5p – the equivalent of about £1 or perhaps, at most, $2 today. I loved every minute. I felt free, in charge of my life, a million miles from the restrictions of school and the London suburbs. I had grown up in a wonderful loving family; but I needed to move on and find my own place in the world.

I spent a few days in Istanbul, wandering the streets and trying to take everything in. I frequented the water-sellers with bright, multi-coloured containers on their backs; listened to street musicians and saw performing bears; found beautiful Islamic art and manuscripts in mosques and museums. I sat by the Galata Bridge watching the fishermen. They kept their fish alive in baskets by the side of their boats, somehow managing to keep their balance in the choppy waters as they weighed them, and then skilfully threw them up to their customers on the wharf above.

Istanbul was not my final destination, however, and soon it was time to move on. As I left Istanbul, the distances between towns increased, and many of the people who gave me lifts were long-distance lorry drivers. Some wanted company, but most, I think, picked me up out of kindness. When you hitch-hike you tend to meet the kinder members of the human race – it's this kindness that prompts them to stop. There was little competition. Most people travelling east were going by train or bus.

I was dropped by a lorry driver a few kilometres outside Turkey's capital Ankara, and asked directions to the city centre at a nearby police station. The ten policemen in the building crowded round, unwilling to let me go; eventually two of them drove me into town, insisting on stopping several times to buy me sweets. It was not the normal image I had of policemen. I was welcomed everywhere in Turkey. Children

played round me in the street and old women grinned at me from windows above. When I asked directions, a crowd of people would gather round, and often someone would walk with me to wherever I was going. If they didn't know where to direct me, they would gesticulate wildly and point in several different directions, leaving me to choose.

I left Ankara, passing the mountain where Noah was supposed to have built his ark, and before long I was approaching Iran. It was a police state where all cafés and public buildings had pictures of the Shah displayed alongside Mohamed. At the border, I had a stroke of luck. Five large trucks returning from Liverpool were waiting there and one of the drivers, nicknamed Fredo, insisted on taking me all the way to Teheran.

It was a two-day journey. We slept under the lorry and stopped to bathe in rivers, which ran cool and clear from the rocky hills in the distance. It was spring; the fruit trees by the side of the road were covered in blossom, and in the fields were medieval-looking, cattle-drawn ploughs.

In Teheran I explored the narrow back-streets and ate raisins, apricots and exciting Iranian dishes from the street-stalls which cluttered the roads and pavements. I discovered a new way of drinking tea. It was poured into small glasses with china saucers (they were, I was told, actually made in China.) You then poured the tea into the saucer and drank from that. Sugar was served in lumps, but you didn't stir them into the tea. You dipped them in, and then held them under your tongue, letting the tea become sweetened as it passed through your mouth.

Several weeks had now passed. Occasionally, I felt homesick for England. I bought Agatha Christie's *Death on the Nile* from a bookstall. Then John Wyndham's *Trouble with Lichen*, which I read avidly – only to find, as I neared the end, that the last ten pages were missing. It was only several months later, back in England, that I was able to obtain another copy and finish it.

I had seen children working in the streets of Turkish and Iranian towns. On the next stretch of the journey, I was given a lift by the driver of a lorry full of melons, who was travelling with his ten-year old son. We arrived late at night at our destination, where the driver, a thin swarthy man with a large moustache, barked out his orders. The boy's job apparently was to unload the lorry, while his father and I went off to a nearby café for a drink.

Twenty minutes later, we suddenly heard the noise of an engine starting up. Having completed his task, the boy had decided to go for a drive in the dark. There was a screech of gears as he turned the lorry round, the sound of a loud engine rumbling gradually into the distance, then – silence. My companion in the café, however, did not seem put out. It was all in a day's work – all part of the boy's training. Ten minutes later the noise of the engine gradually returned. There was another screech of gears and then the lorry appeared, apparently without a driver, heading fast toward us. It suddenly swerved and drew up in front of us at the café. I could just make out a tiny head at the bottom of the windscreen, with a satisfied smile on its face.

As I continued to travel east, the Asian hospitality which eventually led me into fair trade continued. My next lift was from a student who insisted I should stay the night at his house. He was dressed in fashionable western clothes, with thick black hair down to his shoulders. His house, he said, was "very close." His younger brother went on ahead, with our baggage on a donkey. We trudged up a steep and rocky path, into the mountains. The countryside was dry, brown and almost barren. I was beginning to realise what William Blake meant when he wrote about 'England's green and pleasant land.'

Two hours later, a lovely village appeared on the side of the mountain. Every house was the same dry mud-brown colour and blended completely into the background, built by hand with local stone. The floors were of pounded earth and there was no electricity. It was an almost self-sufficient community, only importing items like paraffin for cooking and lighting. I tried to teach my new friend the difference between 'a' and 'an' – a difficult task. The two brothers lived in one room, and after a wonderful meal, we all fell asleep.

Next morning we were up at dawn. We were now walking down from the mountains, and soon reached the road. I was on my way again. Almost every car stopped to offer a lift, and taxis too. By mid-afternoon I was at the border of Afghanistan.

Afghanistan at that time was one of the poorest countries in the world. It still is. If Turkey and Iran had been a culture shock, Afghanistan was like a bombshell. As I entered Herat, the first town of any size, I could see that western fashion was irrelevant here. These were proud people

who had no wish to wear western clothing and for whom religion was an integral and important part of their lives.

In many ways, apart from a number of lorries and a few buses, it was like going back to a different age, to a time when you either had a trade or lived off the land. The taxis were ponies and traps and the boundary between country and town was unclear. Boys walked through the streets guiding herds of sheep or goats; camels carried produce from the countryside for sale in the local markets and shops, or simply on strips of sacking by the side of the road.

It was a far cry from the wasteful economies of Europe. Almost everything was made, bought and sold locally. Metalwork, cooking pots, clothing, furniture – often they were made at the back of the shop and sold at the front. Delivery or collection was by bicycle, camel or cart. Packaging was almost non-existent, and nothing was thrown away if it could possibly be mended. Tailors and shoe-makers sat on the streets, working industriously to give a new lease of life to a shirt or a shoe. If something really was on its last legs, it could still be re-used. Old clothes were stitched together to make patchwork bags or blankets; bicycle parts were re-welded to make a new bicycle. Old rubber tyres were cut up and turned into sandals, old bus frames into buckets or even kitchen sinks.

Today when we see images on television of Afghan men with flowing beards and lined faces, we're inclined to think of religious fanaticism and terrorism. We have been conditioned to categorise people according to their external appearance. The reality is often very different. On my second morning in Herat I left my hotel to look around. An old man with a grey beard greeted me in the street outside. He had a dirty cloth wound round his head, clothes whose colour had become indistinct because they had been washed so often, and a blanket thrown across his shoulders despite the heat. His brown feet seemed to merge with the stone of the ground we were walking on, as if they were a natural part of this dusty landscape. My white skin seemed out of place.

He motioned for me to sit down by the side of the road. Was he too just passing through, a traveller all his life, visiting this town as part of a semi-nomadic lifestyle? Or was he about to kidnap me? I was relieved when out of his backpack came not a gun, for I had seen plenty in the street, but a kettle, cups and a portable cooker. In a few minutes a pot of

tea was brewing. He served it in small cups with no handles, strongly laced with sugar. I could not speak his language and he could not speak mine. It was a meeting of two cultures, two religions, two ages – our backgrounds could not have been more diverse. We spoke in smiles.

My map of Afghanistan described its roads as either 'tarmaced', 'passable' or 'difficult.' The road from Herat to Kabul was 'tarmaced.' The idea of hitching a lift on a bus in Britain is unthinkable, even in the worst of weathers. In Iran and Afghanistan it was different. Cars, buses, lorries, horses and carts – almost all of them stopped. As I journeyed to Kabul, I was dropped by a lorry driver in the middle of the desert. The lorry headed off along a 'passable' road towards a distant village. I wondered what on earth the 'difficult' road must be like. I surveyed the empty landscape around me with some misgivings. Where was I? I put my thumb up, wondering what I would do if I was stranded. The amount of traffic was pitifully small. Ten minutes passed, with nothing at all except a man with two donkeys.

I need not have worried. A bus, rusty and worn but painted in a multitude of bright colours, clattered to a halt beside me, and the driver, a middle-aged man with a deeply lined face, beckoned. I raised my eyebrows enquiringly and pointed to my thumb. "Hitching – you understand?"

The response was a nonchalant shrug, so I raised my eyebrows even further and repeated, "hitching, no money, you understand?"

The deep frown and aggressive expression on the face of the driver was almost as worrying as the idea of getting left on my own in the desert for the night. It was three or four hundred miles to the next town, after all. I didn't want to offend him: the Afghans were a fierce people.

Again the driver shrugged. Then he snapped his head back impatiently. It seemed to be a signal to get on, so I did, somewhat gingerly. I sat down, wondering if I was expected to pay later. The engine started up and we moved on. Eventually I realised that the driver wasn't bothered at all about my money. Gradually, my heart settled down. Driving a car, a lorry, or a bus – it was all the same to him, he was just offering a passing stranger a lift.

It was a ten-hour drive to our next stop, Kandahar, which I remember for a café which I entered because I liked the music being played inside. The proprietor saw me and beamed. A westerner! – now was his chance.

He played two records alternately on his rusty gramophone throughout my meal – *Twinkle, Twinkle, Little Star* and *Old Macdonald Had A Farm*, adapted for Afghani instruments. They were awful.

I walked down a nearby alley, exploring, and found a woman tearing the feathers off a pile of dead sparrows. I was intrigued – was this an Afghan delicacy? Apparently not. In the street nearby her husband was selling fritters made of 'fish.' I didn't try them.

Next day, travelling through the desert towards Kabul in another bus, I witnessed another example of the Afghan bus-drivers' friendliness to strangers. A car had broken down by the side of the road. In England you would just phone the AA or the RAC. In Afghanistan, there aren't many cars and such organisations don't exist – or certainly they didn't when I was there.

So the bus driver stopped. It seemed to be a natural response for him to offer help. We all piled out to examine what the trouble was. The men crowded round, while the few women passengers stood back, chatting. Stoves were brought out and tea was made. Almost everyone seemed to carry a mini kitchen on their backs, as if they knew delays like this would happen, and had come prepared.

We peered at the car. Everyone had a different opinion as to what was wrong, and two men in particular were expressing their views so forcefully that I thought they would come to blows. However, after several experiments and more tea, there was a sudden splutter of life. The car's engine was back in business, and its stranded occupants could resume their journey. We gave it a helpful push, waved farewell, and climbed on the bus again. A few hours later, as the light began to fade, we arrived in Kabul.

Kabul was attractive to hippies in the seventies because drugs were so cheap and readily available there. They were openly sold and used on the street, and several times each day I was offered hashish or heroin. I was not interested. My father had smoked heavily for most of my childhood – cigarettes, that is. He was a typical middle-aged businessman – hair receding, the host of frequent dinner parties and a reluctant weekend mower of the lawn. The thought of him rolling a joint and passing it round is unimaginable. Try to picture Maggie Thatcher and Ted Heath slumped on a beanbag and chilling out with a joint and you'll understand what I mean.

Like many smokers, he went through the cycle of quitting and restarting for many years. The irritable moods were hard for all of us around him to deal with. As a result, I was never tempted to smoke and never got involved with drugs, which was unusual amongst travellers in Afghanistan.

Many years later, in a market in New Delhi, I saw a white-skinned man in rags, hollow-eyed and emaciated. He was an addict, and was begging for a few rupees from the Indians in the street. It wasn't a tourist area, and many of the people passing by were obviously very poor themselves. Somehow, it was more shocking than seeing an Indian beggar, or a beggar at home in Britain.

So I didn't buy drugs on the 'hippy trail' to India. What I did spend money on was some wonderful bags and purses which I saw in Kabul. They were woven with a rich mosaic of natural colours, bright but not synthetic, and were hand-made using whatever material was available at the time; no two were the same. They reminded me of the buses and lorries I had seen on the road, which were painted from front to back in bright primary colours, as if to brighten people's lives as they travelled through the dusty deserts and mountains.

I hadn't seen anything like these bags in Britain, and bought a selection of purses and wallets to take back with me. My rucksack was half empty, after all. I had no idea what I would do with them, but I was sure I would have no problem in selling them. It had nothing to do with fair trade. I just saw a lovely product and knew there would be a market for it in Britain. It was, unknown to me, an almost accidental first venture into the world of handicrafts.

After a few days in Kabul it was time to move on to Pakistan, and then India. I travelled to the Pakistani border on top of a lorry carrying sacks of rice. It was bumpy, but in the open air you could really appreciate the scenery. Mountains soared up around us.

The Pakistani border official was nonplussed when I presented my passport to him.

"No, no," he said, "This is not possible. You are not English."

I was nonplussed myself. "I *am* English," I said, and produced my British flag to prove my point. It had, after all, come in useful.

"You are *not* English," he insisted. "I do not believe you."

I repeated again that I was, indeed, English, and waved the British flag at him meaningfully.

"But this is impossible," he repeated. "You are too *dirty* to be English." I was still covered in dust from my ride through the mountains.

To my surprise, being English was quite an advantage. Once I had established my true identity, the border official could not have been more helpful. I was given a seat and offered tea. I expressed my gratitude profusely.

"No, no, please, there is no mention," I was told. "It is in my disposition, because – you are an English person."

Everyone in Pakistan wanted to practise their English, and they all had particular phrases which they wanted to share.

"This is my father," said a lorry driver as we twisted and turned along the Khyber Pass. He pointed towards his companion, who was, I thought, about ten years younger than him.

"Do you mean your brother?" I asked.

"Yes, yes, my father," was the reply. "Barking dogs never bite." There was a gap in the conversation for a while. Then:

"Barking dogs never bite," he continued, nodding sagely. "Yes, yes," he re-iterated, as if I was an idiot not to understand.

We stopped for a drink and I asked if there was a toilet I could use.

"This is a free place," he said, "Have no regards! Not like England – our country is free. Any place is free for toilet, any place, when you like, it is free. Barking dogs never bite."

The Pakistanis were the most friendly and generous people I had encountered on the whole of my journey so far. In Afghanistan, I sometimes felt people were suspicious of me; at other times, especially in Kabul, I felt they were only interested in my money. I could have passed through Pakistan without spending any money at all. Everywhere, I was offered meals and welcomed.

Religion came up frequently as a topic of conversation with the people I met. One, a Muslim in Lahore, was obviously well-educated. I told him I was a Christian. He was keen to discuss this with me.

"I understand that Jesus was God's son," he said. "So who was God's wife? This I cannot understand."

I could not answer that one. It was too complicated. I decided to ask him the questions.

"What do you think about Hinduism?" I asked.

"Oh, they are all infidels and idol-worshippers," he responded immediately. Then, perhaps, he realised this was not quite the right thing to say. It was not a good idea to appear so intolerant.

"We are all God's children," he continued, "Muslims, Hindus, Christians, we are all equal – we are all manufactured by one God. It is very, very nice to talk to you as brothers of the same faith."

I was looking forward eagerly to seeing India; but it would prove to be impossible to hitch-hike there from Pakistan. The 1971 war between them, which led to the creation of Bangladesh, had only ended a few months before this. It had not made relations between the two countries any easier, and the border between them was closed. To get into India, I had no alternative but to fly. I took the shortest route, with Afghan Airlines from Lahore to Amritsar.

As a fair trade buyer, I have flown to India many times since. It is always exciting to arrive in India, but this first time remains, in my mind, the most exciting of them all. After three months travelling across Europe and Asia, I reached Amritsar in June, 1972. It was a momentous occasion – I had arrived!

After a brief stay in Amritsar, I travelled on to New Delhi, the Indian capital. It was June, the hottest time of the year: the temperature was around 40°C. I hadn't thought of that when I planned my trip. You didn't have to move to start sweating; you just had to be outside. Despite the heat, it was strange and wonderful to be in a thriving city again, after the dry and arid deserts of Afghanistan, Pakistan and the Punjab.

It's hard to imagine the noise, bustle and exuberance of a large Indian city if you haven't been there. The roads were chock-a-block with buses, cars, three-wheelers, scooters, bicycles, rickshaws, vans and lorries of all shapes and sizes. All of them vied for space with buffalo carts, donkeys, the occasional camel and cows which wandered around wherever they liked. 'Horn please,' announced the lorries and buses above their tailboards, and the noise of horns was almost non-stop.

The streets and markets had wonderful displays of foods and dishes, most of which I had never seen or tried before. They entranced me and enticed me with their magical aromas and cheap prices. It all went to my head. I ate dhal, fried meat, yoghurt, in fact any kind of food I fancied

from street sellers and cheap cafés. The heat was intense, and I quenched my thirst by drinking litres of water straight from the tap.

There weren't any Lonely Planet or Rough Guides in those days to tell you how to look after your health, and bottled water was hard to find. My book on survival told me I should boil water before drinking it, but how? It all seemed a big hassle. It looked okay and everyone around me was drinking it.

It was a mistake. I had already had minor gastric problems in Afghanistan and Pakistan. In New Delhi I collapsed with severe dysentery. My trip came to an abrupt end. Within ten days, barely conscious, I was on a plane back to England. My weight had dropped from 10 ¾ to 6 ¾ stone, and apparently I nearly lost my life.

The way the journey ended was unfortunate, but my memories of it, and of the hospitality I received from so many people, had a profound influence on my life.

It was a shock to see the way people live in countries like Afghanistan and India and to compare it with our affluent lifestyles in Britain. The romantic visions of camels in the desert, snake-charmers and marble temples had not disappeared; if anything, they had been enhanced. Yet I had also seen families living in tents by the side of the road, children begging, and women washing their clothes on the pavement. They were struggling to survive, let alone make a decent living.

Being there with them, on the street with all its sounds and smells, is very different from watching news reports about poverty on television. You feel personally involved; you realise these people really are a part of one world.

People with virtually nothing had been generous with what they had. Sometimes I was offered cups of tea or meals; sometimes people just asked me questions and made me feel welcome.

So, when people – like Lynne – ask me how I got into fair trade, I only have to tell them of the kindness and generosity I saw on the hippy trail. I still encounter that kindness and hospitality when I travel abroad today. Sometimes I think that the poorer people are, the more hospitable they can be, and the more generous with the little they have. At the time, I asked myself what I could do to repay this kindness and hospitality. Many years later I found the answer. It was to open a fair trade shop.

4 Action Starts At Home

THE IDEA OF starting a fair trade shop was still a long way off in the future, but the seeds had been planted. I would begin by selling the purses from Afghanistan, and see where that led.

After returning from India, my first priority was to get better. My mother was so glad to have me back that she promised to cook me the most wonderful meal of my life, anything at all I wanted.

"Can I have baked beans on toast, please?" I was in a pretty bad way. I had to eat each bean separately, one at a time. It was a relief, however, to be back home, away from the heat of the Indian summer, and over the next few weeks I made an excellent recovery.

I had spent my childhood in a suburb of London. So it was with some trepidation and much excitement that I travelled 'up north' to start a university course in York in October, 1972. Before this, the furthest north I had been was Norfolk. When I got to York, of course, I found half the students were from the south anyway, so I wasn't out of place. In fact, students with a Yorkshire accent were so rare as to be considered by some to be quaint, and cultivated by others as if they were somehow more 'authentic' or 'real' than the rest of us.

The campus of the University of York is at Heslington, an idyllic spot just outside the city. It was built in the 1960s around a pleasant landscaped lake, and some students rarely venture from it. York itself is a prosperous city, whose economy then revolved largely around tourism; apart from a couple of chocolate factories, little manufacturing industry

was left. Despite its affluence, it still had its problems, and it was in York that my concern for social matters came to the fore. In the seventies the 'big issue' was homelessness.

On my first visit to town I was approached by an elderly man dressed in a dingy cast-off grey suit. He had a ragged beard and unhealthy red cheeks, and had obviously been drinking.

"You're a student, aren't you," he asked, or rather told me, perhaps under the impression that I was not aware of this. Or maybe he was just talking to himself. You could see the thought process going through his mind – "it's a student...new to town...excellent opportunity." It wasn't long before he had persuaded me to give him a few coins.

"Thank you, thank you," he said, shaking my hand, "ye're a good fellow."

The encounter reminded me of the beggars I had seen on my trip to India earlier that year, and the homeless people sleeping on the pavements in New Delhi. I couldn't do much for them. One of the problems of poverty in the Third World (less so since the advent of fair trade) is that it's so hard to know what you can do to help. Perhaps here I could make a difference?

I gathered that several alcoholics in York slept rough and rarely got a decent meal. In fact some of them hardly ate at all. Characters like ex-boxer 'Con' Bailey, covered in scars, and Brian 'Ban the Bomb' McDermott, who was as emaciated as any starving child in Africa, would roam erratically around the streets, occasionally swearing at policemen, or waving a bottle of cider in the air.

"Can yer lend us ten pence for a cup o' tea?" they would growl, putting the coins in a grubby pocket till they had enough for the next bottle of cider or sherry.

If you didn't want to give them money and offered a cup of tea instead, they would still be grateful. Any sympathy was welcome; the streets, though busy, were lonely. They were ignored by most, insulted by a few, and only occasionally treated with kindness.

I became involved in the city's first shelter for the homeless. This was an empty potato warehouse, which was converted into living accommodation for twenty men – ten beds down each side (reminding me of boarding school), a small dining area with chairs and tables, and

a tiny kitchen at the top. There was little funding and food was always a problem. At the end of the day we would scour the market-place for vegetables; stall-holders would throw them away rather than bringing prices down by selling too cheap. We approached local butchers and fishmongers with a cheeky "Anything here that's past its sell-by date?"

The kitchen was bare but its main feature, apart from an ancient cooker, was a huge cauldron. The recipe for cooking was simple; throw it all in, add salt, and let it boil. It was a cross between a soup and a stew, and was different each day according to the ingredients we'd been given. The human contact that the shelter provided was as important as the food, though. For many, it became a home. They knew that a few people were prepared to do something to show they cared, and were willing to treat them as individuals, not just as 'alcoholics' or 'beggars.'

From involvement in the local shelter for the homeless I became aware of homeless issues more generally. I learned at the shelter that the local council had plans to demolish a number of terraced streets, whilst at the same time, there was a long waiting list for accommodation. A number of council houses had been left empty for years with no attempt to renovate them. This seemed illogical, unjust and, in a word, stupid, especially as some of these houses were not even in demolition areas. I could not solve the problems of poverty in the Third World, but here, I thought, there was something I could do to make a difference.

I was studying English, but what good was this doing to solve the world's problems? After my second year at university I dropped out and moved with two fellow activists into a council house which had been empty for many years. Number 17, Dove Street was just outside York's historic city wall, and York Squatters' Association was now formally in business. It was soon headline news in the local press, and furious debates took place at council meetings, with Councillor John Clout, the Conservative Party chairman, claiming that it was 'unfair' on those who were patiently waiting on the council's housing list; we were jumping the queue.

However, the press was sympathetic. "Families and individuals," it reported, "are being forced to walk the streets by day, while sleeping in bed-and-breakfast hotels, bus shelters or the railway station by night." The 'hotels' were not the sort you would spend a holiday in. One man's

'bed' had been in a shared bathroom, on a board above the bath. But the council's Housing Committee was determined that all squatters be evicted and that the demolitions go ahead.

To the dismay of some councillors, there was a legal process which still had to be followed. The council could not just send in the bailiffs and throw us out. However, their solicitors were unprepared, and had little or no experience in this area. After a few weeks, notices were served, requiring us to move out immediately, or we would be taken to court.

Initially, we were alarmed – as was intended. Squatting, though, is a civil, not a criminal offence: we were not being prosecuted. We read the wording carefully. The documents were full of errors and omissions! We went to court, defending ourselves on the basis of the most obvious error – the council had made no attempt to discover our names. The case was instantly dismissed. It took a few weeks for the council's solicitors to ask us who we were. Having done so, they took us to court again. Then for the second time, the case was thrown out, on another legal technicality.

On the third hearing, the solicitors got their paperwork right, and the council could now evict us. We weren't, as Councillor Clout claimed, trying to jump the housing queue (which he acknowledged was a long one.) We were simply trying to bring the issue to the public's attention. So we moved out of Dove Street, and into another empty house, in Sydney Street, a terrace on the other side of York. The legal process had to begin all over again.

Understandably, this made some councillors extremely annoyed. The publicity in the local press, however, was having an effect. Within a couple of weeks, nine houses had been occupied by squatters – five in Sydney Street and four elsewhere. Squatting doesn't mean squalor, though: in many ways, we made the properties more habitable, and the locals were happy to have us. Most of the squatters were families or single parents with young children. The council's response when families became homeless was to put them into the most basic bed and breakfast accommodation. They had to roam the streets, with their children, during the daytime.

The solicitors were more experienced by now, making fewer errors, and we were running out of legal technicalities. We defended ourselves

on the grounds that the council had no suitable accommodation for the families with children, but in April 1975, we were all ordered out.

The local paper – now clearly on our side – turned its attention to the arguments we had used in court. There was nowhere for the families to go, and the emergency accommodation available for homeless families was a disgrace. It consisted of two small terraced houses, one of which already housed 21 people, mostly children, one family to a room. Instead of 'SQUATTERS EVICTED', the A-boards outside newsagents around town declared 'YORK HOMELESS LIVING IN GHETTOES' and quoted my arguments in court that conditions at the council's emergency accommodation were "absolutely disgusting:"

"In one house there were three families with five children living in three rooms and sharing a kitchen and bathroom. In the kitchen there were two rusty old ovens, which took an hour to heat, and a window in the bathroom had been missing for six weeks.

"The toilet was so filthy that most people used a public one. In December [the author] believed everyone living in the two houses had scabies. One of the occupants had apparently tried to commit suicide three times in the last three months, and most were on nerve tablets. One woman told [the author] she had had to throw out two wet mattresses. A rat kept her and her children awake at night."

The story was picked up by national newspapers and made the national news on the BBC and other channels.

To keep up the pressure, two of us moved into another empty council house nearby. The council was fed up, and decided on different tactics. Instead of going to court, they sent the bailiffs down with a policeman. The council workmen were in a difficult position. The council workmen, instructed by Mr Hugh Jones, the Housing Estates Manager, to smash the front window, were in a difficult position, because I was standing in front of it. I explained that the council would be acting illegally if they used force to enter the house. This got nowhere. So, with youthful ebullience, I shouted to the waiting press and onlookers, "Smash the council, not this house!"

At this stage the policeman decided it was time for him to intervene. In a reasonable voice, he tried to persuade me to move. I knew that if I did, the windows would be smashed and the house would be made uninhabitable.

So I refused, repeating that it was the council and the Housing Estates Officer who were acting illegally, not me. Unfortunately, the forces of law and order were on the side of the council. I was arrested.

A month later, I was charged in the criminal court with having acted "in a noisy, turbulent, and disorderly manner, to the annoyance of Mr Hugh Jones, in breach of the peace." I assumed that Mr Jones would not do me any favours in court, but I was wrong.

"Were you annoyed by Mr Piercy's conduct?" asked my solicitor.

"Well, no," responded Mr Jones, to everyone's surprise – not least my own.

"I don't want to be legalistic," continued my solicitor, "but the charge does say that Mr Piercy *annoyed* you."

"I wasn't annoyed," replied Mr Jones. "He was just stopping my workmen from doing their job."

Whether Mr Jones secretly supported our campaign against the council, I will probably never know, but I owe him my thanks. I was acquitted.

In many of the poorer nations of the world, homelessness is a very big problem indeed. Young people in the countryside often move to the cities, hoping to improve their lot and make a better living for themselves. Many cities are bursting at the seams with people searching for work and trying to find somewhere to live. In Indian cities, you see tents by the side of the road made from sacking, tarpaulin and plastic sheets. At first you think they are for storing the wares of street sellers, or perhaps building materials. Then you see children playing nearby, and clothes hanging out to dry on nearby branches or fences. The makeshift tents are people's homes. Often they belong to families who have moved to the city in search of better prospects.

Millions more live in shanty towns, but they have no security. If the local authority wants to develop the area, they are often just thrown out and the bulldozers move in. Squatters' rights, if they exist at all, are usually meaningless in the face of corruption. A small bribe will ensure that the police do nothing to prevent the forcible eviction of unwanted tenants, legal or illegal.

Were all the court hearings in York a waste of public money? Councillor Clout and his cronies undoubtedly thought they were. Yet the squatting campaign had the intended effect. It created publicity in the press,

which spurred York council on to action. Some streets were saved from demolition and renovated, and the council's emergency accommodation was improved.

17 Dove Street is now a desirable residence. According to a local estate agent, it could fetch up to a quarter of a million pounds if placed on the market today. And Sydney Street? It was demolished. The houses in the terrace next to it are now much sought after. I now live in one of them, although no longer as a squatter – I own it. Several times a year I receive letters from property agents, trying to persuade me to sell.

5 Wearing Badges Is Not Enough

AFTER BEING EVICTED from Sydney Street, I found rented accommodation, and went back to university to complete my degree course. The months of serious studying which followed did not lessen my ideals, however. A normal career held no interest for me; I wanted to do something useful, to change the world. It was 1976, and young people didn't just dream of a better world; we really thought we could help to make it happen.

When I finished my degree, fair trade was in its infancy, more of an idea than a reality. It wasn't a viable option in terms of making a living. I was attracted to retailing but there were hardly any fair trade goods to sell. So I entered the world of books. I wanted to challenge conventional ideas, to encourage people to think.

I had discovered a late-night café called Gumbo in Vanbrugh College at the University of York. It was run by volunteers and provided vegetarian food at cheap prices, such as bean stew for 8p and wholemeal bread for 1½p.

The word 'alternative' became a buzz word in the 1970s. 'Alternative lifestyles' were all the rage. Some people started living in communes and tried to be self-sufficient. The organic food movement started to blossom. It became fashionable to be vegetarian. I avoided meat anyway; I didn't have much money – and didn't know how to cook it.

Now I started to read about the connections between western ways of life and the Third World: that to produce 1lb of beef, for instance, you

have to feed the animal 10lb of grain. Europe imports grain from Third World countries to feed its livestock, while many people in the world are struggling to get enough of the basics. The idea that eating meat might lead to food shortages in other countries was new to me, and I decided to give up meat completely.

That was thirty years ago. Today there is even more demand for the world's resources. The world's population has doubled, yet markets dictate that land is given over for growing bio-fuels. The pressure on land increases as developing countries, and especially China, adopt the lifestyles of the west, especially a meat-rich diet. In India, too, the middle class is growing. Demand is increasing and global food prices are rising.

"In Britain," says Harriet Lamb of the Fair Trade Foundation, "we only spend 20% of our income, on average, on food; but in developing countries, people spend anything from 50 to 80% of their incomes on it. Rising food prices for them are a disaster."

It's an issue which will bring fair trade and the environmental movements closer together. Fair traders are concerned about poverty and environmental problems are making poverty worse.

It was at Gumbo, which served as a meeting place for like-minded individuals, that I met two fellow students, Nick Witt and Judy Gibson, and we started talking about 'alternative' books.

"It's ridiculous," we said, "loads of new books are being published about the environment, feminism, politics, all kinds of 'alternative' ideas – but you can't buy any of them in York. None of the normal bookshops want to stock them. You have to travel to Leeds to find a vegetarian cookbook!"

Like most graduates, we were wondering what to do with our lives.

"Why don't we start an 'alternative' bookshop," we asked, "selling all the books that no-one else is willing to stock?"

We began with bookstalls at the university, selling everything from Marx and Engels to Rachel Carson's environmental classic *Silent Spring* to comics like the *Fabulous Furry Freak Brothers*. We didn't care what people bought if it helped to build up our stock and our capital. Another graduate, Tony Zurbrugg, joined us, and we started searching for a suitable premises.

Eventually we found it – a dilapidated shop in Walmgate, just inside the city walls on the east side of York. Crucially, because we expected students to be a large part of our custom, it was on the route between the city centre and the university. By the spring of 1977 we had raised enough to buy the shop outright. It cost £5,500.

It was in a terrible state, far worse than the houses I had squatted in, and we spent months renovating it. The floor had to be dug out, damp walls re-plastered, everything rewired – it was quite a challenge. We were completely unconcerned about health and safety; Nick and Judy removed several large sheets of asbestos from the back room by hand. But we had the confidence of youth. I had just obtained a degree in English literature; now I learnt the arts of plumbing and how to use a blowtorch. Although it was hard work, there was always the Spread Eagle, a real ale pub across the road, to look forward to at the end of the day.

Finally, in August 1977, York Community Bookshop opened. In the spirit of the times, it was a co-operative. We held lengthy meetings each week to discuss finance, display, promotions and every other detail of running the shop. Even more time was spent discussing our social aims. Which publishers and titles should we stock? Were they too radical or obscure? Should we sell books on how to grow cannabis? Should we stock books by feminist or black authors if they had right-wing political views?

It seems unbelievable looking back, but at that time, none of the bookshops in York had any books about the environment. They had nothing about alternative medicine, hardly anything about yoga, and if you found a novel by an author from Asia, Africa or South America, you were lucky indeed. They wouldn't touch anything by gay writers or about gay politics – it was far too controversial. They had nothing from the Virago or Womens Press, soon to become mainstream publishers. We were the only shop in York selling books by Maya Angelou, Kate Millett and other writers who today appear on the A-Level curriculum.

We had hit upon one of the secrets of successful retailing – to sell something that customers want, which they can't get anywhere else. Judy was excellent at doing the accounts, Nick liked being busy selling, and my own strength was sourcing new titles. Tony's forte was discussing

politics; we had to make it clear when we'd had enough. We made a great team. It was an excellent lesson in retailing, which I discovered I loved.

We were also top class in another area that makes for retail success – enthusiasm. We weren't concerned about money; none of us wanted to make a fortune. We paid ourselves £14 a week, which was roughly what we would have received on Social Security. We believed in what we were doing for its own sake.

Our customers could see this, and came back for more. We knew our stock well and if someone wanted something, we knew where to look; we would search out books and pamphlets from publishers across the country, and some from abroad. We exchanged views with customers on whatever topic was to hand, and continued to widen our range of stock.

At the time York Community Bookshop opened, it was fashionable to show people where you stood. We bought a machine to make badges, and had a colourful selection for all tastes. For animal lovers there was 'Don't Badger The Badger' and 'Only Rotters Hunt Otters.' For anti-nuke protesters we had 'Nuclear Power – Stick It Up Your Uranium' and for pacifists 'Protest and Survive' and 'Better Red Than Dead.' The 1970s were a time of industrial action, and for left-wing activists we had 'Help The Police – Beat Yourself Up' and 'Batchelors Peas On Its Workers.'

For those who were tired of politics there was 'Don't Vote – It Only Encourages Them' and 'Whoever You Vote For, The Government Gets In.' For grown-up children we had 'We Are The People Our Parents Warned Us Against.'

We even had a badge for people who disapproved of badges – 'Wearing Badges Is Not Enough.'

We realised that without our customers, whatever their views, we couldn't survive. It seems fairly obvious that you should treat customers with respect, but there are still plenty of businesses that aren't very good at it. "I think our customer care was exceptional because of our idealism," Nick told me recently. "It was instinctive for us because we had built up the business from scratch and really believed in it." If Councillor Clout had come in looking for a book on housing, we would have done our best to find it for him. Perhaps he did.

When you have a passionate ideal and you try to turn it into a business, you sometimes concentrate on the ideals and neglect the bottom line. It's a pitfall that many 'ethical' retailers fall into, including some fair trade shops today. No-one in business can neglect the balance sheet. Judy, Nick, Tony and I knew we had to make the business pay its way.

If you have high ideals, you can become arrogant, thinking you're right, and everyone else is wrong. You may start dividing your customers into those who sympathise with your views, and those who don't. Unfortunately, something like this happened at York Community Bookshop. It was successful, and was attracting a lot of customers, but its founders were getting itchy feet. Within three years Judy, Nick, Tony and I had all moved on to other things.

We had been joined by a 'second wave' of staff – Sarah, Bob and Jane – who initially worked for free as a kind of apprenticeship, before being paid. As the founders left, a 'third wave' came in, who expected to get paid from day one.

By then, however, the shop was starting to struggle. Competition was growing and sales were going down. Some of the later staff may have seen the shop as infallible because of its earlier success, not realising that businesses have to change and adapt if they are to survive. They were all women with strong feminist views. Instead of broadening the shop's appeal and trying to attract different customers, they appealed for help to the people who were already supporting them. Promoting the shop as a radical feminist co-operative had the opposite effect from that intended: it put some of their customers off.

"I used to shop at YCB a lot," a friend later told me. "But in the end I just didn't feel welcome and stopped going in. None of the staff smiled at me. It felt like they wanted all their customers to be women."

York Community Bookshop closed in 1985. Like many fair trade shops today, it was not in a good location. Threatened by competition from large bookshop chains, it did exactly what some fair trade shops are doing today as they are threatened by competition from the supermarkets. It turned inwards, appealing to its core customers because of its worthy aims. It could have survived for longer if it had broadened its appeal to a wider range of people.

How do fair trade shops relate to their customers? Generally, I think,

very well. Their staff are usually committed, friendly, and welcoming, because they're keen to promote fair trade to as many people as possible. In fact, if you're not a 'believer' you're often more welcome than those who are already converted to the cause. The logic of fair trade is simple: more customers means more sales, which brings more benefits to producers.

6 The Wilderness Years

AFTER LEAVING YORK Community Bookshop, I visited India again briefly, went trekking in Nepal with a friend, and came back to England full of enthusiasm to start a fair trade shop. It was 1980, and I cycled to Harrogate to attend one of Traidcraft's first meetings. Its purpose was to whip up support and discuss Traidcraft's plans for the future. I began to get really excited, but I wasn't sure if Traidcraft's products would be enough. I looked for other suppliers, and couldn't find anything much at all. There were just a few odd products sold by campaigns and charities.

I was also concerned about margins – the amount of profit you make on the goods you sell. Were the discounts offered by Traidcraft viable? I realised they were aiming their sales pitch not at wholesale customers, but at fair trade enthusiasts who would sell their products on a voluntary basis. It didn't look as if it would be possible to run a Traidcraft shop and earn a living from it.

So instead of fair trade, I got into self-development. I wanted to understand my past, so I could understand myself better and grow. A friend recommended re-evaluation co-counselling.

"It's very different from normal psychiatry, where you go and see a shrink, who helps you sort your problems out," he said. "Co-counselling assumes that we all have problems; we're all human and none of us is perfect. You work in pairs; one person is the 'counselled' and the other

is the 'counsellor.' After an agreed length of time, you swap roles; the 'counsellor' becomes the 'counselled', and vice-versa." This sounded interesting – I had never liked the idea of one person being better than another.

"As counsellor," my friend went on, "your job is to listen, and maybe ask the occasional question to help, if the person you're counselling seems to be stuck. You never pass judgement or make suggestions as to what they should do. It's their time and they decide how to use it." I decided to join a local group.

In the first session I discovered another tenet of co-counselling, that nearly everyone has a poor opinion of themselves – we all think we're unintelligent, unattractive, unable to get on with people – or whatever. "The aim of co-counselling," we were told, "is to build up self-confidence and help us realise that life is not bad or good, it's what you make of it. So we always end a session by affirming something positive about ourselves or our lives."

Feminism was strong at that time and women were saying that men need to cry. In my first co-counselling sessions, I explored my childhood at home, and couldn't find much to get worked up about. In my urge to be politically correct I tried desperately to cry. But the tears just wouldn't come.

When I talked about school, it was a different matter. At eight years old, I was sent to boarding school. My father had gone to the same school thirty years previously. He had loved it and assumed that I would love it, too.

It was my first week. I sat at breakfast, at the 'bottom' table presided over by the Matron. She had crinkly hair and a permanent look of displeasure on her face. The food arrived – cold stewed tomatoes on soggy fried bread – ugh! As the boys around me were getting up to leave, I was still struggling to swallow my first mouthful. 'Revolting' was not a strong enough word to describe it.

"You can stay here till you've finished it!" said Matron.

I would have eaten the most unfairly traded food imaginable if it had been available as an alternative.

The headmaster of the school was a vicar and should not have been. He was a bully. H.M., as he was known, was a short man, but heavily

built, like a rugby prop forward. He was in his fifties, with an aggressive skinhead haircut, and grey hair which went well with his grey suits. It made his red face stand out all the more when he lost his temper. He was feared by everyone.

He taught Latin. We took it in turns to translate texts from Caesar and other authors, starting with the boy at the top of the class. My heart began to pound, harder and harder. Would the bell ring before it was my turn? But of course it never did.

"Piercy," H.M. said, "your turn!" His apparent lack of emotion belied the deep anger that always seemed to lie not far below the surface, ready to explode at the slightest provocation.

"Um," I started, "um, the horse, um, the horse of the general, um…" I paused, aware of the growing frown on H.M.'s forehead. "Um, walked…"

"What was that?" he asked in an ominously quiet tone of voice, which I recognised as the calm before the storm. "Walked, did you say?" I searched desperately for some other meaning, but could think of none.

"Idiot!" H.M shouted, the frown deepening on his forehead. "Do people gallop, or canter, or trot? How many times do I have to tell you that horses don't walk! How many times!" By now I was terrified, because he was standing in front of my desk, hands on hips, staring at me malevolently, his whole body infuriated. "Use your brain, boy, if you have one!" he continued. Then suddenly, he turned round, shaking his head, as if he was saying to himself, "How much longer can I stand it, teaching these half-witted morons?" But all that came out, in a resigned sort of voice, was "Next!" My turn was over.

The threat of a beating was never far away. The school was run on fear.

This was in the mid 1960s. Now it was 1982. I was nearly thirty, and I was sitting on a cushion on the floor, shaking at the memory. It gradually eased. My twenty minutes was coming to an end. "Do you want to finish with something positive?" my counsellor asked.

"Well, I do have a happy memory from school," I said. "Whenever H.M. walked into a room, there was always instant silence, we were so afraid of him. But his wife was different. She was a quiet, gentle kind of woman. Sometimes she used to stand at the bottom of her garden, next

to the school playground, and give us all Quality Street sweets. It was as if she was apologising for her husband's behaviour. "I'm sorry I can't change him," she seemed to be saying, "but at least I can do something to show that someone cares." I've associated Quality Street with that memory ever since.

The counselling continued, and other demons climbed out of the box. I realised I was afraid of relationships. Why? I went back to my past to try to find the answer.

Once again I was at boarding school. I was twelve, and I was the darling of my English teacher, because I had won a couple of prizes in national poetry-writing competitions. He was a wonderful teacher, perhaps the best I ever had; he loved his subject and inspired us all. He encouraged us to write honestly and without restraint, to express our feelings, to find our creative talent.

But there was a darker side to his character, which I had submerged in my mind. So far in fact that I was totally unaware of it, until it suddenly leapt out again in counselling. He was a paedophile.

He had started inviting me to his room, at the top of an old oast house which was now used mainly for music lessons, and was often empty. It was in an isolated part of the school grounds, next to a horse chestnut tree wood where we used to play conkers. For the past three years he had been a stickler for discipline; his stern voice in the corridors, "Silence!", commanded instant obedience. Now he was offering me sherry in his room. We read poetry, discussed Ted Hughes, Adrian Henri and other modern poets. I was flattered that this teacher, whom I admired and looked up to, felt me worthy of his personal attention.

But after a few visits the subject changed from poetry to other matters.

"Do you know about sex?" he would ask. "Would you like me to take my clothes off? I'd be very happy to, if you'd like me to. You could take your clothes off too, if you want to."

This was pretty scary. I couldn't just laugh and say, "No thanks, I'm not in the mood today," or "Well, I think I'd prefer to talk about T.S. Eliot, actually."

I stuttered, "No, it's okay thanks." And at that point our meeting usually came to an end.

But eventually he couldn't hold on any longer. One afternoon, he suddenly lunged out at me, pulled me on to the floor, shoved his large hand up my shorts and grabbed me round the crotch.

He was a powerful man, with a huge chest, as befitted his former occupation; he had been a captain in the Royal Navy. I struggled to escape. He was lying on top of me, with his hand up my pants. And then suddenly, he came to his senses. Or had he had an orgasm and that was it? Whatever the reason, he stood up and allowed me to leave.

It was a minor incident, perhaps, but very scary at the time. There was no-one to talk to about it – how many boys of this age want to talk to adults about sex, anyway? And physical assault, or the threat of it, was part of the culture of the school. So I buried the whole thing in the back of my mind.

Almost twenty years later, it re-emerged from its hiding place. I was shaking with fear, and holding on to my counsellor for support. Over a period of months, this gradually changed. Instead of shaking, I started banging cushions in anger. In the end the emotions died down; I was able to accept, and eventually forgive. I can think of this teacher now with equanimity. He was an excellent man in many ways, and at least he didn't go any further than he did.

I may have got off lightly. Antony Worrall Thompson, who attended the same school, relates far worse abuse taking place in his autobiography *Raw*, including oral, anal and group sex. This was with children aged only 11, 12 and 13. Behind a cloak of respectability, the school was a pretty frightening place.

It was at this age, about twelve, that my epilepsy grew worse. I had 'grand mal' attacks soon after waking up, which put me out of action for the rest of the day. I would regain consciousness with a splitting headache, go to bed, sleep for a few hours, and be back to normal by next day.

This happened about once a month throughout my childhood and early

twenties. But as I delved into my past through co-counselling, the pattern changed. The attacks came more frequently. I started having them every week, and then almost every day. I tried acupuncture, meditated, went on fasts for up to ten days at a time, and tried giving up medication altogether, which probably just made things worse. Starting a fair trade shop became an impractical dream. It was a difficult period in my life; I fluctuated between depression and optimism. I felt confused, uncertain and insecure, and sometimes had two or three epileptic attacks in a single day. For six long years, I was unemployed and unemployable, but I still clutched on to hope. I wrote in my diary, "Sometimes I feel that all my friends and loved ones have left me and no longer care. What God seems to be saying is that the tears, the anger, the upsets are all strong and real, but will not last."

My grandmother, who had died a few years before, kept appearing in my mind, smiling at me. She hadn't smiled much in her life; my chief memory of her was at Christmas parties, when she would bang on the table to demand attention. "Don't be so stupid!" she would tell my uncles, and insist that everyone listen to her. Now she was smiling constantly at me, and seemed to be telling me confidently, "you have the power that is in all of us to make things happen, to express yourself, to love and receive love. You're going through a difficult time, but don't worry, you will come through in the end." Sometimes she was so close that I could have been talking to her face to face.

In December 1985 I went to stay with my parents in Kent for a few weeks. I don't remember much about this period; I was only half conscious for much of the time. The one clear memory is of feeling annoyed with my father.

"Good morning, how are you?" he would ask as I came down to breakfast. "Did you sleep well?" Further questions followed. His intent was kindly – but I just wanted to eat my breakfast. Today, if my own children come down to breakfast looking tired and grumpy, I have to stop myself from doing the same. They too have made it clear that they just want to eat their cereal. If you're not a morning person, you'll understand.

After about ten weeks at my parents' house, I had an epileptic attack which just went on and on. I was unconscious for two days. On 7 March,

I woke up to find myself in Guy's Hospital in London, where I'd been taken in an ambulance. For the second time in my life, I was apparently close to death.

It turned out to be the first step in reclaiming my life. I was put on a new drug, carbomazepine, which stopped the epileptic attacks, and without any noticeable side-effects. Within a couple of days I was awake and alert, and a few days later I was cooking a meal for everyone on the ward. I was given some money to buy food from the high street below, and made a respectable lentil stew. Today, we live in such a nanny state that I doubt if that would be allowed.

Cooking that meal was a great form of therapy; it gave me a sense of purpose again. It wasn't just good to get out of bed: it was great to feel that my mind was lucid again, that I was capable of doing something constructive and actually enjoying it! My future lay before me – what to do next? There were no doubts in my mind. I was determined to investigate fair trade again, and find out if things had changed since that meeting in Harrogate six years previously. This time, my dream of a fair trade shop would become a reality.

Above My mother at the Ecoffins warehouse.
Below left Weaving a bamboo coffin in China.
Below right William Wainman.

Above Richard Adams at Traidcraft's warehouse, mid-80s
Opposite page Oxfam's first shop, Oxford, early 1950s.
Below right Local dignitaries open Justicia, Bolton, arriving on a rickshaw.
Below left Siesta, Canterbury.

Council will act on six York squatters

YORK CITY COUNCIL is to begin legal procedure to move squatters from two houses in the city.

The houses are: 17 Dove Street, which is being occupied by four young men; and 1 Emily Street which, as reported in Saturday's Evening Press, is now occupied by an expectant mother and her three-year-old daughter.

The council's Housing Services Committee unanimously decided last night at a meeting in the Guildhall, to empower the sub-committee which dealt with an earlier case of squatting in August to deal with these instances on similar lines.

But they hope the squatters will go and take no council representations before measures like eviction are necessary.

FIRM STAND

"It was unanimously decided," said the committee chairman, Coun. John Clark, "that the council should take a firm stand against any unauthorised entries into their properties, though we mean to go and take to talk to the people involved and find a solution before resorting to eviction.

"But we cannot allow this to prevail or it will proliferate throughout the city and before very long I think it is open to people who are pulling quickest and waiting their turn.

"We understand that the person involved in Emily Street came to York from away, and that his family are prepared to provide a home for her."

At 17 Dove Street, which has been occupied for about three weeks, the front garden is tangled and overgrown. Panes of glass are missing and tatted across the front windows. There is no action at the back.

WARNING

The front door bears a hand-printed notice headed "Legal Warning."

This says: "This property has been occupied by squatters and trespassers. We are in possession and we intend to stay here. If you try to evict us with force we will prosecute you. You must deal with us through the courts.

"It goes on to quote from the 'Statute of Forcible Entry Act 1381'."

A spokesman for the Housing Department says that 17 Dove Street was bought by York Corporation several years ago. It was one of several very poor properties excluded from compulsory purchase under during the Nunnery Lane area redevelopment, because there were one or two other houses in the street in very good condition.

The corporation had tenants in No. 17, but had to take them out because of the internal conditions of the house.

NEIGHBOURS

Neighbours in Dove Street are divided in their reactions to the squatting.

Mrs. Agnes Rawley, who lives at 24 Dove Street with her husband and two children in their own house, says the squatters are quiet and make no disturbance, and she would rather see someone in the house than have it empty.

Miss Irene Hope, of 20 Dove Street, a council tenant, also said the squatters have no nuisance, but she felt it was wrong that they should be there jumping the housing queue.

She was rehoused from a private tenancy, also in Dove Street, and found her private landlords less restrictive. That house was demolished for the redevelopment.

Three of the four squatters of 17 Dove street. They refused to disclose their names.

Left Homelessness in York: a bigger problem than most people realised. Within a few months, over eight homes were occupied by squatters, mostly children with young families.

Yorkshire Evening Press, Friday, November 22, 1974 11

Jeremy Piercy, Julie Fish, centre and Helen Power, three York students brave the rain in King's Square, York, today, to bring attention to the plight of Vietnam. They are members of Third Way in Vietnam, a Birmingham-based group which has launched a fund to help the 550,000 war orphans of Vietnam. The group has about 100 supporters in York, many of whom, like Jeremy, Julie and Helen will take part in sponsored 48-hour fasts this week.

Right Student activist: fasting for peace in Vietnam, 1974.

Opposite After three court hearings, the police were sent in. I am third from left, bowing my head.

Right
"Smash the council, not this house!" I was arrested and charged with a breach of the peace.
Left
Was I "stopping the workmen from doing their job"? Sydney Street and several adjoining streets were later demolished.

Above
York Community Bookshop, with a huge range of badges in front of the counter.

Right
Another trend at the time was to reuse envelope labels...

Below ...a trend that was still popular when One World opened in 1986.

Above
Darjeeling, 1980.

Left
The Wilderness Years.

Below
50p(aisa) is worth about 2p - enough then to buy a simple meal of rice and lentils. Would you bother to pick up 2p if you saw it lying on the pavement?

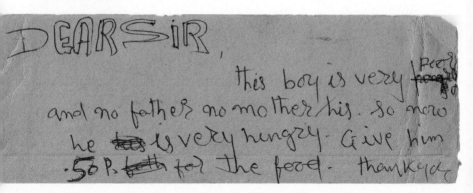

DEAR SIR, this boy is very ~~poor food~~ and no father no mother his. So now he ~~has~~ is very hungry. Give him .50 P. ~~both for~~ for the food. thankyou

Above A dream comes true: One World opens, 1986.
Below From the outside: York's first fair trade shop!

Above We expand. Leeds branch opens, 1988 - Liz on the left.
Below Manchester shop opens, 1990. Rumillajta - a popular South American band at the time - liven things up.

Left Stuart, our first buyer, relaxes in India with Leeds shop manager Jayne.

Below "They're earthy, vibrant, creative..." - but will they sell?

Above Our warehouse fills with carvings and Kisii stone from Kenya.
Inset Kenyan woodcarver.

Above Dr Correa, Ambassador of Ecuador, admires a balsa wood parrot - Wakefield, 1990.

Below right One World, Wakefield - a disaster.

Below left Local dignitaries cut the tape at our Birmingham shop, October 1992.

Above Staff meal above the shop in Goodramgate, York 1990.
Below Bradford shop, 1990. We change our name to Shared Earth. To the left is Debbie
Fletcher, now our longest-serving member of staff and manager of our Leeds branch.

Left
Kisii stone from Kenya at our Manchester shop, 1992.

Right
Manchester staff, 1992.

Left
Parrots and toucans - will they fall over? Birmingham shop, 1992.

Above We move our Goodramgate shop to an excellent new location on Minster Gates, which all the tourists in York pass.

Above Judy Byford, the designer of our popular Animal Magic range.

Above Some of Judy's designs on T-shirts imported from Asha Handicrafts in India.

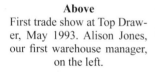

Above
First trade show at Top Drawer, May 1993. Alison Jones, our first warehouse manager, on the left.

Above
Two of our wholesale stalwarts, Matt and Kevin.

Left
We capture America: Animal Magic at the New York Stationery Show, 1995.

Above
The 'baggers' making Animal Magic sets in our warehouse. All the paper was 100% post-consumer waste.

Below
Tourism Employer of the Year Award. With Alison Hammond, who worked in our Birmingham store.

Below
With Hugh Bailey, MP for York, at the Tourism Employer Awards.

7 One World

THERE WEREN'T ANY books about how to open a fair trade shop, so I would have to work a great many things out on my own. This time it was serious; I really believed it could work. I was itching to go. After a week in Guy's Hospital, and with the new pills controlling my epilepsy, I was fully fit.

Traidcraft had come a long way since the meeting I had attended in Harrogate in 1980. They weren't just selling tea, coffee and jute baskets anymore. Now they had rugs, toys, jewellery and a variety of homeware and kitchenware, as well as a bigger selection of food and recycled paper. Mo Fini's venture, Tumi, was also beginning to wholesale an excellent range of crafts from South America. The One World Shop had opened, along with Justicia and World Of Difference, and Traidcraft's four stores were thriving. Clearly, there were enough fair trade products available to make a shop work.

However, doubts still remained. Could a fair trade shop work as a business?

Many of the new shops had started as stalls in churches. Often the people who ran them were either retired, or had a partner with another source of income. Although they were extremely committed to fair trade, they only wanted to work part-time, and didn't need, expect or want to get paid for it. In business terms, they wanted to minimise risks, costs and financial commitment. So the first fair trade shops opened in the cheapest and therefore worst locations. If they were anywhere near the

high street it was usually in the basement of a church or as a concession in a Christian bookshop.

How would people find them? Most fair trade shops thought customers would go out of their way to come to them, because of what they were doing. In theory, they wanted to promote fair trade to as many people as possible. In practice, they relied on people who were already converted to the cause – the 'beard and sandals brigade.' This is still the case with many fair trade shops today, and it limits the ability of the fair trade movement to give larger orders to the producers. This isn't a criticism, because the people who started these shops, and their customers, have shown enormous commitment; without them the growth of fair trade in the UK would not have been possible. It's just sad that more fair trade shops are not on the high street, where fair trade's powerful message and wonderful products are easily visible to everyday shoppers.

I came from a different starting point. I wanted to make a living from fair trade. I wanted to make fair trade products available to as many people as possible, which would create more work for the producers, and raise the profile of fair trade too.

I wanted to prove that a fair trade shop could work – that you could trade fairly and run a business too. The ultimate aim of the fair trade movement is that all trade should be fair. A successful shop would prove to other retailers that it's possible to trade fairly and still make a profit. This, I believed, would encourage them to switch to fair trade. After all, no-one wants to exploit producers just for the sake of it. It happens because exploiting people leads to cheaper prices, which – according to traditional reasoning – brings in more customers. If there's an alternative, though, and they can still make a profit, then there's no reason why retailers should not choose the ethical option, especially if they think this will attract more people to shop with them.

Today, the ground rules are changing; economic theory is being turned on its head. Businesses used to be judged by the way they treated shareholders, customers and (occasionally) staff. Now some are facing scrutiny for the way they treat their suppliers and the environment. When we see cheap prices, we are suspicious, and not just because we think the products may fall apart after a couple of months. Cheap prices are being associated with both sweatshop labour and with damage to the planet.

However, back in 1986, this was all a long way ahead. There was no guarantee that a fair trade shop could make a profit. I was just trying to open a little shop in a city in the north of England.

My first task was to think of a name. It had to stand for my beliefs, and attract people in too.

"Why don't you call it Hungry for Change?" suggested a friend. It was the name of a local development action group with which I had been involved. But it smacked too much of charity.

"I like the idea," I said. "But there's too much guilt in it. It implies that people are hungry or starving, and you need to help them. I'm not trying to attract donations. I want to run a business which will work because people like the products, not buy them because they think they ought to. And I also think that if we create jobs abroad, which are fairly paid, there won't be so much hunger in the first place. So much poverty in the world is due to unjust trading relationships between the rich and poor countries of the world."

I wanted a name which showed that the way we live in one part of the world affects how people live in another, and that we're all people, no matter what our cultures, religious beliefs or economic circumstances. A name that showed that trading which makes one person a millionaire at the expense of others who starve is wrong.

"We need a change of heart," I told my friend. "We need to realise that we are all one in the world, and we will never be truly happy if others are suffering because of the way we live our lives. In fair trade, trade becomes something of mutual benefit, not just a means to get rich at the expense of others."

Another idea I had was to call the shop Fifty Paisa. In 1980 a small boy in New Delhi, about seven or eight years old, had given me a scrap of cardboard with the message:

DEAR SIR. This boy is very poor and no father no mother his. So now he is very hungry. Give him 50 paisa for the food. Thank you.

Fifty paisa (half a rupee) was worth about two pence, enough at the time to buy a basic meal of rice and dhal. It shocked me and made me question our values in Britain. Would I bother to pick up 2p if I saw it lying on the pavement? "A lot of people," I said to my friend, "seem to have jobs which they don't really enjoy. Sometimes it seems like their

main objective at work is just to increase their pay – which then gets spent on things they don't need or even want."

It's unlikely that the boy who gave me this message wrote it himself. He was probably 'owned' by a gang run by an older child – perhaps thirteen or fourteen years old – to whom he would be responsible for handing over his 'takings' at the end of each day. In return, he would receive a place to sleep, in a room with ten or twenty other children, and a simple meal of the sort which would keep him alive so he could continue begging, but would not be enough to make him look anything other than starving. Similar gangs are common in most Third World cities, run by older children who are involved in begging, stealing and child prostitution.

Although the name Fifty Paisa held a great deal of personal resonance for me, it too smacked of charity. It was also too obscure. You already know that I run Shared Earth; it might surprise you to know that in 1986, I decided to call the shop One World. It reminded me of my first trip to India where I learnt that regardless of circumstances, we were all people. The name One World also had environmental associations that appealed. We only have one planet, and we need to respect it.

I now had a great idea, a great name, and plenty of enthusiasm. Unfortunately, this wasn't enough to start a business. I had to face the problem almost every new business faces – money. For the last six years, I had lived a simple lifestyle and put a small part of my Social Security payments into a savings account. I ate brown rice and lentils, wore jumpers to reduce heating bills, hitch-hiked or cycled – it was partly concern about the environment, and partly the subconscious motivation that eventually, I would succeed in fulfilling my dream of opening a shop, and would need all the savings I could get to do so.

I had also started busking. I played the concertina and sang old English folk songs, which were much loved by the American tourists who flock to York. I was staggered by some of the donations I received. I had heard that musicians and street artists commute from Leeds to York to busk, and now I could see why. It wasn't just Americans and other tourists;

even local people contributed – and not just with money. I went into the market one morning to buy some carrots and potatoes. The stall-holder peered at me.

"Are you the lad who sings whaling songs down Petergate?" he enquired in a broad Yorkshire accent, frowning at me.

What was the problem? Had I offended him? Was he a closet animal rights activist? I cautiously admitted that I did.

"I don't want yer money. 'Ave 'em for free," he said, handing the vegetables over.

The frown was still on his face. He clearly didn't want to be accused of sentimentality.

For those who may be questioning my credentials as an environmentalist, whaling songs chronicle the trials of the British whalers of the eighteenth and early nineteenth centuries. Their ordeals were as bad as those of any sweatshop worker in India today. They were often in open boats in the Arctic for fifteen or twenty hours at a time, and suffered from frostbite, atrocious food and appalling living conditions. Many of them died. After months at sea they'd arrive back in Liverpool, Whitby or other ports, flush with money, which would soon disappear in a spree of drinking and revelling. Penniless, they would then be forced to re-enlist in another long trip.

I was more careful with my money, and by 1986 had several thousand pounds in the bank. My parents also helped. They were delighted that I had recovered from epilepsy, and although they had misgivings about whether a fair trade shop would work, they generously agreed to give me a small loan to get it going.

I spent hours doing cash flow projections and profit-and-loss forecasts. Stock would be the main cost, so I planned to open in the autumn. In the gift trade, about 25% of annual sales occur in the five weeks before Christmas; December sales are usually four times as high as any other month. The profit from Christmas sales, I reasoned, would pay for the initial stock and see me through the lean months of winter.

I also needed staff. All fair trade shops at the time relied on volunteers, and I decided I would have to do the same, at least to get everything off the ground. It wasn't ideal, as there is a downside to relying on volunteers. They often work infrequent hours, or leave after a few months and never

get to know the stock properly. They may never gain the skills to re-merchandise displays or replace stock. Some volunteers, though, are excellent – dedicated, knowledgeable and great with customers. I would have to rely on volunteers until I could afford to pay staff, if this crazy idea ever took off.

I had lived in York a long time and had built up a lot of friends and acquaintances. But epilepsy had affected my memory. The last six years were almost a blank; I felt as if I'd been away from York for three lifetimes, not three months. It was like beginning my life from scratch. I searched through my old address book and started visiting people to rebuild friendships and associations, and to build a team of people who could help me start One World. But I was struggling to remember who people were. How did I know him? Who on earth was she?

One friend was Sue, but I couldn't for the life of me put a face to her name. I phoned her up anyway, and she asked me for coffee. I knew her name, because it was in my address book, next to the address I was visiting. But how did I know her? I tried to work it out as we sat there chatting. It was a strange feeling; I just couldn't remember. Then, as I got up to go, she touched me gently on the shoulder. Everything came flooding back: she had been my girlfriend. The mind is a funny and terrifying thing. It was as if the wonderful times we'd had together were encapsulated in a single, magical moment, and a simple touch brought them all to life again.

All I needed now was the shop itself. The question was, where? It's a well-known catch phrase that 'location is everything' in retail. I had seen what happened at York Community Bookshop when the competition intensifies: unless you're in a niche market, the shop in the high street always wins out. I couldn't afford the 'real' high street, alongside the national chains and supermarkets, but I didn't want to be in a little back street where only the dedicated few (those with beards and sandals) would come. I was looking, in the terminology of the estate agents, for a 'good secondary site.'

It wasn't long before an excellent position turned up. It was on

Goodramgate, a curving medieval street just inside the city walls. A large number of pedestrians entering the city from the north pass down it on their way into town. It was occupied by Alison Holmes Décor, a gift shop selling collectibles. They were moving to a better location near the Shambles, which almost every tourist visits, but was far too expensive for me at that time.

Mr Holmes looked at me doubtfully, and asked what kind of shop I was intending to open.

"Fair trade?" he said. "Do you mean free trade?" I tried to explain.

"Oh," he said. "Well – I see." He was clearly not impressed.

Mr Holmes had six branches around Yorkshire and was doing well. You could see how his mind was working. "Well, I've got another young idealist here, with another crackpot idea that won't work. It might last a year, maybe two if he's lucky. But who knows? It's not my business, and if the landlord is prepared to take the risk, and I can get rid of my lease, then what happens to him is not my problem." He agreed to go ahead.

I had to pay a premium for the lease, which ate into my cash reserves, but finally, after a few weeks, the lease was signed. The key to 17 Goodramgate was in my hand! It was one of the most exciting moments in my life, only to be surpassed by the opening of the shop a couple of weeks later. I hurriedly phoned up all the people who had offered help and told them this fantastic news – and gently reminded them that their services would soon be required. Sue's two daughters, Hannah and Naomi, who were in their teens, were enthusiastic helpers at One World. Right from the start, the shop appealed to young people, and was staffed by them too.

Mr Holmes had generously agreed to leave behind his old shop-fittings, which were well suited to the goods I would be selling. A few repairs were needed, but nothing substantial, particularly when compared to the renovations York Community Bookshop had needed. The shop-front was painted, a sign put up, leaflets printed to spread the word – York's first fair trade shop was about to open!

Meanwhile, I was contacting suppliers, discussing terms, and placing orders. The most important supplier was Traidcraft. In fact, when it first opened, the shop had hardly anything else apart from Traidcraft products. I had visited their shop in Newcastle; now I was keen to start selling their products myself.

They were almost the only fair trade wholesaler in the UK at the time, but their terms to retailers were not helpful. To get a commercial discount, you had to order in quantities of ten, the only exceptions being a few extremely expensive products such as large rugs and coffee tables. My attempts to persuade them to be more flexible – by reducing the minimum order to five, for instance – were unsuccessful. They didn't know who I was and weren't prepared to budge. So I took the plunge: I ordered one of each of all the expensive items, and ten of everything else.

This was fine with some products, like painted elephants and parrots, which we re-ordered again and again. Some, however, did not fare so well, especially the things that were supposed to be practical, rather than ornamental. Some people in the fair trade movement felt that the products we sold should serve a purpose; luxuries to put on your mantelpiece were inappropriate, they said, when there was so much poverty in the world.

I could see their point, but to me that wasn't the issue. The aim was not to tell people they should be living simpler lifestyles because other people were poor. It was to provide fairly paid work for producers who would otherwise be unemployed or exploited. The aim was to bring them up, not bring ourselves down. As in any other business, if customers didn't want the products, what was the point in trying to sell them?

I soon had a plethora of tea pot cosies, shoe shine sets, wooden trays and pin cushions, all of which I was desperate to shift. The worst products were table napkins. They came in five different colour combinations, so I had ordered fifty in total. We still had nearly fifty, two years later.

That first order in 1986 was massive. A few days after the lease was signed, an apparently never-ending stream of boxes arrived, till the whole of the back of the shop was filled to overflowing. My helpers – like the retired Pat McWeeny, and Alice and Beccy, two girls from the local Steiner School – were invaluable. I worked into the small hours to get everything unpacked, checked, priced and on to the shelves, and eventually, exhausted but exhilarated, crawled into my sleeping bag in the storeroom.

One World opened on 10 November, 1986. There was no fanfare or cutting of tape. I just opened the door and waited. Would anyone come

in? To allay my worries, I got on with unpacking and pricing; so many goods had arrived that there was still lots to do.

I was so pleased when someone came in – a potential customer! – that I almost hugged them. It wasn't a friend wishing me well, either. It was someone who had never heard of fair trade, but who liked the window display, and decided to investigate. Soon helpers and well-wishers were arriving, not quite in droves, but the shop was full and the atmosphere was carnival-like. Coffee from Nicaragua was served, along with local biscuits. The shop was open at last! It was the culmination of many years' dreams, hopes and worries.

Positive comments continued throughout the day. "Ooh, this is a nice shop – have you been here long?" (We still occasionally get asked the same question today, twenty-three years later.) It was wonderful to hear. I enthused to everyone about fair trade, how it made a difference to people's lives, and how the shop had only just opened. Most people bought something, even if just to show that they wished me well. Enthusiasm is catching.

Traidcraft's products dominated the shop at first. They were mostly plain coloured, earthy, natural – shelf after shelf contained jute baskets and sikas from Bangladesh. They were soon joined by a selection of crafts from Tumi – animals made from gourds, intricate mirrors, and brightly painted parrots and toucans, carved from balsa wood. Some were tiny, others several feet tall, and every one was different. They contained every colour in the rainbow, with bright reds and blues predominating.

A few shops in York sold Asian crafts – Indian bedspreads, bags and the like – but these parrots were like something out of a South American fairy tale. They conjured up images of naked Indians in the Amazon jungle, exotic wildlife, wild rivers and Incan priests. Nothing like them had been seen before in York. Their only problem was their weight. Balsa wood is so light that they over-balanced at the slightest touch, especially the toucans, which had long protruding beaks at the top, and small bases below. When a large one tipped over, it scattered all the smaller birds beneath it, just as large trees do to the smaller trees beneath them when they're felled in the Amazon rainforest.

Most of our sales were more mundane, usually small items such as cards, little baskets and packets of coffee and tea. There was no

competition from the supermarkets which had yet to discover fair trade. Fair trade coffee was hard to find in 1986, but that's not surprising considering how awful it tasted.

The lease I had signed included a small flat above the shop, so I moved in and gave up my bed-sit on the outskirts of York. As sales grew, living space began to shrink, taken over by boxes of stock. There wasn't an office – the office was the counter. I was in the shop six days a week (hardly any shops opened on Sundays then) and, if I wasn't on the shop floor, I'd be behind the till, dealing with the paperwork in between serving customers. The files were on a shelf behind the counter, and I placed orders by looking round the shop to see what was missing. Today, it's all done by computer.

Starting a new business is risky. It usually takes time to get on to its feet, and often you only start making a profit after a couple of years – if you haven't already gone bust, that is. The shops in secondary locations in any town will give you the picture. They come and go like a flock of migrating birds. About half of all new businesses fail within the first three years.

When One World opened, I had no idea how it would do. I was full of optimism, and I had a lot of drive to make it work – I believed passionately in what I was doing. I'd visited other fair trade shops and tried to learn from them. It's always easier to see the mistakes others make (and try to avoid them) than to see your own shortcomings. I'd also done my best to plan ahead, and tried to be cautious with my financial predictions.

I had forecast that the first year's sales would be £36,000, and that I would make a loss of £15,000. So imagine my surprise and delight when I discovered at the end of the year that I had sold £64,000, and instead of making a loss, had made a profit of £3,000! My living expenses had to come out of this, of course, and profit doesn't relate to how much money you actually have in the bank. I was still heavily reliant on a bank overdraft: but I was doing well. The shop was popular with a wide variety of passers-by; it wasn't just a magnet for fair trade enthusiasts.

I realised this one day when a sales rep parked his car on the double

yellow lines outside the front door. He was showing me his catalogue when a policeman walked in. He came straight to the counter.

"Oh dear, trouble," I thought. "What have I done now?" I had been moved on for protesting against the Vietnam War, arrested for giving out leaflets to soldiers during the British Withdrawal from Northern Ireland Campaign, and taken to court for squatting and protesting against the local council. Policemen and I hadn't always got along. This time, however, it wasn't me in trouble.

"I do beg your pardon, Officer," said the sales rep, "I'm only in here for a few minutes. I'll move it straight away. Honestly, it won't happen again."

But the sales rep wasn't in trouble either.

"Er, that's ok, don't worry," replied the policeman, who was so tall he towered over both of us. He looked a bit embarrassed. "Actually," he continued, addressing me, "I just wondered if you've still got any of those multi-coloured Peruvian hats you had a few months ago? You know, the ones with ear-flaps?" Unfortunately, we had sold out. But the tension eased, and I promised to save him one next time they came in.

Not many people in York knew about fair trade, and One World was a puzzle for some, with its strange mixture of food, books, cards and crafts. Apart from the normal requests for maps of York, headache pills and camera film, which every retailer in a tourist city expects, we were asked for everything from jampot lids, watch straps and tobacco to magnifying glasses, books on fly-fishing and whips.

"I don't suppose you sell lino-cutting equipment, do you?" asked one customer expectantly. "No? Oh well, just thought I'd ask."

Even if customers weren't interested in fair trade, they liked our products, which no other retailers in York were selling. I had found a gap in the market, and business continued to thrive. Sales in the second year grew 60% to £110,000 and, to my astonishment, profit increased to £22,000. It was a clear sign that the fair trade concept worked and I was over the moon.

I was ambitious, confident, and keen to promote fair trade further, so

I decided to expand. In October 1988, I opened a second branch in the Merrion Centre in Leeds.

"Well done – you seem to be doing well," said Mr Holmes, who also had a shop there, in a slightly surprised tone of voice. His congratulations were genuine – he had struggled to make it himself, and was pleased to see me doing well.

There was already a fair trade shop in Leeds, run by Traidcraft, but it was very small, some distance away and located in the basement of the SPCK bookshop. This restricted its customers largely to the Christians who used the bookshop and a few fair trade enthusiasts. One World's new branch appealed to students and local office workers and was successful from the start. My aim was to match York's turnover in the first year. It did so in its first nine weeks! At Christmas, the queues went right to the back of the shop, and the shelves emptied as fast as they could be filled up. It was a retailer's dream. Products like Kisii stone and ebony carvings from Kenya, which had never been seen before in Leeds, were especially popular.

By this time, I had married Liz, who had been a volunteer in York since soon after I opened there. She joined me as a partner in the business, and in September 1989 we opened a third branch in Darley Street, Bradford. In our third year profit increased to £53,000, and in our fourth year, with sales soaring, we did even better, making over £100,000. I could scarcely believe it.

Unfortunately, it didn't seem to make much difference to our bank balance. Over £100,000 was invested in stock and shop-fittings, and the business now had to provide for the two of us, including mortgage payments on our new house, as the flat above the York shop was too full of boxes to accommodate us any more.

As we expanded, we started paying some of our staff. Liz, previously a medical secretary with the NHS, was now managing our Leeds branch, but when our Bradford shop opened, it was clear that another manager would be needed. I came up with an excellent idea, but it was turned down emphatically.

"Having a second wife is not an option," I was told.

Extra staff were also needed in York, because I was spending more and more time travelling between the branches. It was also harder to find

volunteers in Leeds and Bradford, where I had fewer personal contacts. Staffing was a problem.

We had already taken on our first paid sales assistant in York. Chris Stringer had been a volunteer since we opened, and was much more tactful than I was at telling customers that we didn't appreciate them eating ice-cream or smoking on the premises. "Why can't they learn?" I complained impatiently, forgetting it was different people each time. In Leeds and Bradford we paid some staff right from the start. It was tricky – some people were being paid and some were not. Eventually, I took the vital step towards proving a fair trade shop could work, and decided to pay all our staff.

Financially, it was a hard decision to take; the wages bill is the top expense for most retailers. But I wanted to prove that fair trade was a practical option for any retailer, and this wouldn't be possible if we continued to rely on volunteers. There were other benefits, too. Volunteers usually came in only once a week or fortnight, so most of them never really got to know the stock. When we started paying staff, we found that stock control, display and customer care all improved.

In order to pay everyone, savings had to be made in other areas. We had to take a more commercial approach with our suppliers. Traidcraft – even when you bought in units of ten – still offered a very poor discount, and we weren't making the margins on their products that we needed, especially on food. So we started buying less from Traidcraft and more from Tumi and other small suppliers whose wholesale prices allowed for better margins, such as One Village in Oxford and the Coach House in Glasgow. This allowed us to increase our profits and pay our staff.

But disaster was on the horizon. We were now doing so well that I grew over-confident.

All three shops were forging ahead and there seemed to be no barrier to further expansion, other than lack of capital. Despite excellent sales, our overdraft at the bank never seemed to go down, and our bank manager always had a worried expression on his face.

"Every time I see you," he said, "you want more money. It can't go on indefinitely, you know."

It was true. Our profits kept going up, but each time we opened a new shop, the cost of repairs, fittings, stock and legal expenses approached forty or fifty thousand pounds – and all the profit vanished. We couldn't rely on finding a Mr Holmes each time who would leave behind all the fittings we needed.

The obvious answer for expansion was franchising. Franchisees own their own businesses and are responsible for all the up-front costs. If we could attract franchisees, they would pay the legal fees, sign the leases with the landlords, and even pay us for the privilege of using our name. In return, we would give them a proven business concept, unique products and systems, advice and back-up. It appeared to be an ideal solution.

I knew hardly anything about franchising; in fact I was a complete novice. So I called in a consultant to guide us through the process. Like our bank manager, he wore a smart suit, but instead of looking worried, he was all smiles and encouragement. He seemed to know everything there was to know about franchising; he oozed confidence. He flattered us and said what a brilliant and unique idea we had, what wonderful products. On his first visit he pored over the glass counter of our shop in York, examining the silver jewellery from Mexico and Peru.

"Some of these designs are just wonderful," he said. "Do you mind if I have a look at that brooch?" It was the most expensive piece of jewellery we had, pure silver, and priced at over fifty pounds.

"This is absolutely perfect," he continued, holding the brooch up to the light, "it's just what I want for my wife's birthday next week. I'll take it!"

It was a good sale – we didn't often sell items at that price. We climbed the stairs to what used to be my flat, but was now our office. There he confirmed that franchising was an excellent way to expand rapidly; but, he said, good marketing was essential to getting a franchise off its feet.

"I know just the right person," he told us. "He specialises in marketing for new franchisors and he's excellent. I know him well – you can trust him one hundred percent."

A visit was arranged, and in due course our consultant's colleague arrived. He too was dressed in an expensive smart suit. He pored over the counter.

"These designs are wonderful," he said. "That necklace is fantastic. Would you mind getting it out so I can have a look?" It was our most expensive necklace, again priced at over fifty pounds.

"Oh, this is wonderful!" he said, holding the necklace up to the light. "I'll take it!"

I can't remember whether it was his wife's birthday the following week, too, but the effect of the two transactions was to bolster my confidence beyond all reasonable limits. How could we fail, if these well-dressed consultants loved our products so much?

'Handicraft Shops for One World,' declared David Thurlow in *The Times* above a photo of Liz and me fondling a balsa wood parrot. The future seemed unlimited. "Our target is forty shops by 1995," I declared ambitiously.

Ethnic crafts were unusual at the time, and we had diversified into African as well as South American and Asian designs. "You know, I don't think you can go wrong, with these products," our consultant said. "You've got a really unique proposition here. The idea of fair trade is great. And your products are such good quality that I think you could open a shop in a large village and make it work.

"What you need to do," our consultant continued, "is to set up a pilot project in a town which has a different customer base. Somewhere which doesn't have as many students and tourists as York and Leeds. That will give you a better idea about how far you can grow the franchise in the future. Whether you'll be able to open two hundred or four hundred stores, for instance. I'd suggest somewhere close by so you can monitor it easily. How about Wakefield?"

I'd never been to Wakefield before, but now I couldn't wait to get on the train. Within a few weeks, I had signed a lease for a shop in the city centre.

It's always a worry when you open a new shop in a new town. Our first three shops had been a huge success. Wakefield was a different story. It opened with a bang – and closed with a whimper. Immediately after we received the keys, things began to go wrong. We discovered that rogue traders had broken into the shop and were selling cheap T-shirts there. We had to take legal action to get them out, which wasted a week. Then we pushed on with repairs and shop-fitting, and on 20 October, 1990, our fourth branch opened with press cameras flashing.

The Ambassador of Ecuador, Dr Jose Antonio Correa, travelled up from London to cut the tape, and to see our balsa wood parrots, which were carved in Ecuador. I introduced him briefly, but I hadn't done my homework properly, and went on to make an embarrassing blunder in front of the assembled crowd.

"I'd like to extend the warmest welcome to you, Dr Correa, and thank you sincerely for coming," I said. "You have some wonderful crafts in Ecuador. I know it's hard to export when you're enclosed by land and don't have a port, but I think you're doing a fantastic job with these balsa wood parrots and toucans. They're really great and I'm sure we'll be able to sell lots of them in our new shop here in Wakefield."

"Thank you, thank you," responded Dr Correa. "I appreciate your kind words. It's true; we do have some wonderful crafts in Ecuador, and many more apart from these parrots, which I hope you'll consider selling too.

"But actually, we have a long coastline and more than one port. So exporting is not a problem for us. Anyway, I'm very pleased you like our products, and I wish you the very best for your new shop." The clapping and cheers could not hide my discomfort.

We sold several parrots that first week, but the overall sales were worrying. I put this down to a slow start. As the word spread, more customers would come in, I reasoned. I said the same after the second week, and again after the third, but I was beginning to dread seeing the sales figures each Monday. It was becoming harder and harder to convince myself that things would improve.

At the end of December the truth had to be faced. Christmas sales had been poor and it was clear that the new shop was going to make a substantial loss. By now the whole country was suffering from a serious recession, and this could put the whole business under threat. The hoped-for sales of expensive jewellery had not materialised. "Perhaps we should have opened in a large village instead," I joked with a grimace. Our well-meaning franchise consultants were nowhere to be seen; we had to cut costs, and their expensive fees were the first to go.

Any hopes of opening forty shops in five years faded rapidly into the distance. As for four hundred in rural towns and villages – how could I ever have been seduced by such unrealistic fantasies?

It would not have been quite so bad if we only had the crisis in Wakefield to deal with, but in my zeal to expand, I had opened another branch in Manchester. I had a feeling from the start that this shop would do well. Manchester was a big city, had no other fair trade shop, and had thousands of students and young people who we were sure would like our products. We had also found a good location, on a busy thoroughfare, at a surprisingly low rent. Within two or three weeks, it was clear that we were on to a winner.

However, opening both shops at the same time had stretched our cash flow to the limit. The costs of stock and shop-fittings were enormous, and now we had the bleak winter months to get through, when sales are poor but all the bills still have to be paid. It was a disaster. If you have had serious financial worry in your life, or you are under threat of losing your business or your job, you will know how I felt.

I sat at home in despair. "There's no way we can get through this," I said. "We just can't continue. There's no alternative – we'll have to close the business." It was as if all the successes of the last four years had been a mere bubble, which had suddenly burst, leaving nothing. There was a feeling of impending doom – bankruptcy was only an inch away. At the end of the year we found we had made a horrendous loss; all our profits to date had been wiped out by this one big blunder.

All successful entrepreneurs take risks – they wouldn't be entrepreneurs if they didn't. Sometimes it's just luck that pulls you through, sometimes it's luck that puts you under. I resolved to do all I possibly could to avert disaster.

I needed someone with a sound business head and a great deal of experience. I had met Tim Damer on Mrs Thatcher's Enterprise Allowance Scheme. It was instantly obvious that he was especially good at 'people skills' – judging how staff would react in different situations, whether they were suitable for promotion, what training they needed and so on. Apart from anything else, I needed a shoulder to cry on – and Tim was an excellent listener. So I asked him to come in and give us some advice.

He confirmed what we already knew – we needed to cut costs, improve

margins, negotiate with the bank and our suppliers, and ride out the storm as best we could.

As 1990 went by, I became an expert at apologising to suppliers for paying invoices late. But we were still hanging on. It was a struggle, but as time went by, and we still hadn't gone under, I gradually became more confident. As Christmas approached, I knew we had made it. We were over the worst; we would survive.

8 Animal Magic

I HAVE ALWAYS been passionate about the environment. I loved animals and wildlife as a child, and spent much of my holidays wandering the woods and commons near my home, looking for birds, insects and wild flowers. "What do you want to be when you grow up?" It's a question every child is asked. My answer was "an entomologist." This made me feel superior, because hardly anyone knew what an entomologist was. But it was a sincere ambition at the time. The idea of working in an office running a retail gift business would have appalled me.

When I was squatting I met some colourful characters who made a living by stripping empty houses of their lead and copper and taking them to the scrap merchants for recycling. Apart from the legal aspects of this – it was totally illegal – it made sense. Why demolish a house, I thought, and throw everything on to a landfill site?

Later, at York Community Bookshop, I met people who had 'gone back to the land' to live more simple lifestyles. 'Self-sufficiency' was a buzzword in those days, and I had friends who were growing their own vegetables, even rearing goats and chickens and experimenting with solar panels and alternative energy.

I tried to simplify my own lifestyle; after seeing how people lived in India and Pakistan it seemed only right. I stopped eating meat, tried to minimise waste and became a keen advocate of recycling. Selling was in my blood, and after leaving the bookshop, I moved from recycling things myself, like bottles, to selling things that other people had recycled. In

the late seventies, I set up a stall in the courtyard of another popular co-operative, a wholefood bakery, shop and workshop for the disabled – the Gillygate Wholefood Bakery. Here I sold recycled paper from Friends of the Earth, labels for recycling envelopes and other similar products.

It was partly through my interest in recycling that I discovered fair trade. Traidcraft had an excellent range of recycled writing sets and notebooks. Their jute products were completely sustainable, too; the equivalent in the UK would have been making crafts from grass-cuttings from your lawn. I was immensely excited by this. Fair trade seemed to combine two of my greatest ideals: helping people in the Third World, and doing something to benefit the environment. The idea that I could make a living from something I really believed in was almost too good to be true.

As One World got off the ground, my passion almost got the better of me. *"The environment,"* I wrote in a customer newsletter in 1989,

is a global, not a local issue. Dangerous chemicals and medicines, banned here, are sold off to the Third World. Waste is dumped. Rainforests are destroyed to obtain our burgers. Huge profits are made selling arms to both sides in Third World wars. The north, believing that growth can go on forever, encourages a lifestyle based on consumerism. This is a lifestyle that the planet cannot sustain.

Most of this is just as true today, if not more so. A fair trade shop, however, has to sell things people want, not just campaign or try to convert people to its cause. I wanted One World to be a gift shop. That meant selling birthday and greetings cards; but I couldn't find anyone who supplied cards made with recycled paper. In order to complete its range, Traidcraft was buying foods on the open market which were not fairly traded at the time. In a similar way, I decided to stock commercial cards. At least then customers could come to us and buy a gift and a card together; otherwise they might go elsewhere and no fair trade sale would be made at all.

By 1990, we had become Shared Earth. The name One World had been fine initially, but we were expanding and had five shops. There

was also a One World Shop in Edinburgh, a One World wholesaler selling crystals, and One World Week, which caused confusion amongst customers. The crunch came when we opened in Manchester. The One World Development Centre, in a nearby back-street, was mostly an information centre, but also sold packets of fair trade tea, coffee and a few other items.

When we opened, with the same name as them, they were furious, so we decided to change our name. This was a real dilemma; the name One World meant a lot to me. It expressed everything I wanted the business to represent – fair trade, the environment, people of different races, cultures and beliefs all living and working together on one planet. And I just couldn't think of an alternative.

So I organised a competition. I promised £10 to the person – staff, customer or friend – who could come up with the best alternative. There were more than a hundred entries; some people sent in over a dozen suggestions. Some were good; others not. We were never going to call ourselves The Bing-Bong-Bang Parrot Shop or The Fairest Fair Trade And Environmentally-Friendly Shop Of Them All. In the end we weeded the suggestions down to half a dozen and Shared Earth became the winner. It seemed very strange to start with. Now it's hard to imagine anything else.

The One World Development Centre in Manchester closed down a few years later. The sign outside is completely different now. It's a sex shop.

One World or Shared Earth, the name didn't matter – the lack of recycled cards was still a problem. There are three basic types of paper you can use for printing. Worst, from an environmental point of view, is paper made from trees from unmanaged forests – you don't know where it's from or what's involved. The use of trees from managed forests is much better. Usually this is certified with the FSC (Forest Stewardship Council) logo. FSC-certified paper does not contribute to global forest destruction. However, the manufacturing process is still energy intensive and produces considerable volumes of polluting waste.

Best of all is recycled paper. Significantly less energy is used to produce it. It reduces the amount of waste going to landfill, in turn reducing methane emissions which contribute to global warming. It's important, too, to 'close the loop' – most of us recycle our newspapers nowadays, but where do they all go? Without a demand for recycled products, the materials collected for recycling can't be recycled.

In 1991 I teamed up with Judy Byford, a talented designer from Bradford, to produce a set of cards made from recycled paper. The theme was to be the peoples, wildlife and landscapes of different countries around the world. I was somewhat naïve in my initial approach.

"Hi, Judy," I said, "we've got five brilliant fair trade shops and we're really keen on the environment. Would you be able to do some designs for us without charging so we can see if there's a market for recycled cards?"

There was a pause at the other end of the line.

"Well, it sounds a lovely idea," said Judy. "But I'm a commercial designer. That's how I make my living. It takes me a day or two to produce each design. So I can't just do them for free. It would be like you giving the goods in your shops away to your customers without charging them."

"Oh," I replied. "I see." Paying a professional designer, as well as printing costs, would mean a considerable investment. I'd already discovered we would have to print at least 24,000 cards to make a print-run viable, and that would be expensive. I'd never done anything like this before. I was used to ordering in threes, sixes or – if a card looked promising – a full dozen.

However, Judy's imaginative style had captivated me. It was unlike anything on the market at the time. I love a challenge, and this was the early nineties, when green issues were on everyone's agenda. I sensed a commercial opportunity, and decided to go ahead. Shared Earth became a wholesaler almost by accident. Our wholesale department, which today has an annual turnover of a million pounds, began with this range of eight cards.

Once they were printed, we had to sell them, and we couldn't sell them all in our own shops. I started by phoning up all the fair trade shops I knew.

"How many would you like to order?" I asked, before they had agreed to order at all. I assumed they would be interested. Sure enough, the pages of my new order book soon began to fill up; the cards were flying out.

It was a fantastic feeling to see our own, unique designs on the card shelves in our shops. Customers loved the new cards and they were selling fast. I realised that we needed more designs. I was beginning to realise, too, how much people love cuddly animals; the cards with animals on them were selling much better than the ones with people. So I extended the range to sixteen, and followed it up with a new Animal Magic range. Our attempt to become the first serious wholesaler of recycled cards in the UK was really starting to get off the ground.

The Animal Magic range was an immediate hit, and our office – which not long before had been my bedroom – was becoming quite frenzied.

"All in all it's quite pleasant if you wear earplugs and aren't frightened of disorganised chaos," commented one member of staff. In a bid to reduce packaging, we offered a choice to customers – they could either have cards unbagged, or have them cello-wrapped at a slightly higher price. Customers would phone up asking for "twenty wrapped frogs" or "ten unwrapped parrots."

We were receiving some excellent feedback and our new wholesale customers were re-ordering again and again, especially the animal designs. But there was always one suggestion that kept recurring.

"Why haven't you got a cat in the range?" people asked every two or three days.

"Well, there are lots of cards with cats on them in other shops," I said. "I want us to do something different. And there *is* a card with tigers." It sounded a bit feeble; I realised I was making excuses. Perhaps Judy was just a dog person.

In retail, it's always better to find out what customers want, rather than tell them what they want. I decided to take their advice. Soon we had sixteen more cards – including dolphins, puffins, ladybirds – and three cat designs. One became a bestseller, and was reprinted four times.

We soon expanded from cards into gift-wrap and stationery, using the same Animal Magic designs, and with everything printed on 100% recycled paper. We exhibited at trade shows; Top Drawer in London

was our first, followed by the Spring and Autumn Fairs at the NEC in Birmingham and the New York Stationery Show. Within two years we had over five hundred customers, including distributors in the USA, Japan and several European countries.

With crafts, environmental issues are often not quite so clear, especially when transportation over long distances is involved. I was keen, however, that Shared Earth should start buying directly from abroad, and in 1989 appointed our first buyer, Stuart Browning, for this purpose. Full of energy, ideas and enthusiasm, he was not a conventional interviewee.

"He must have been good," commented one of our staff in a surprised tone of voice. "He wore a lime green shirt and a pink jacket – and still got the job."

Most of the time Stuart was a great person to work with, but like all people bursting with ideas, he had some that were excellent, and some that were not. Sometimes he became quite frustrated when they weren't accepted.

"We *have* to do this," he would say, "it's *obvious*. You'll be *mad* if you don't take up this opportunity." He would shake his head in exasperation, as if I was an idiot.

Part of his job was sourcing new suppliers at trade shows. He was committed to fair trade but wasn't too bothered about the bills.

"Buying… it's a push-over," he told our staff. "You just pop down to one of those 'trade show thingies' with as much money as you can get off Jeremy and buy everything you like."

Stuart was the first person to travel abroad on behalf of Shared Earth to source products directly from producer groups. In 1990 he flew to Kenya, Malawi and Zimbabwe with Desmond Abrahams, our York shop manager, who was from Zimbabwe himself. They soon found there was a delicate balance to maintain between the environment and the people who need jobs and income. This was especially the case with woodcarvings, as Stuart indicated in his report on the trip:

The main danger to ebony seems to be in Tanzania, where it is cut down in large quantities and then sent to Kenya. In Malawi, the

number of carvers is tiny in comparison, and replanting projects do exist (we saw large plantations outside Blantyre guarded by soldiers and police.) The carvers have to buy permits from the government for each tree they cut down, though it must be admitted there are large tracks of countryside which are beyond the rule of law; but the amount of wood used for carving is tiny. The situation is totally different from that in the rainforests of South America, where huge areas are torn down to provide land for grazing cattle.

Stuart arrived in Zimbabwe with Des on the day Nelson Mandela made his big freedom speech in Harare, and placed orders for several crates of ceramics, masks and woodcarvings. Next they travelled to Malawi, one of the poorest countries in the world, where they teamed up with a small enterprise development agency and met an unemployed potter, Paul Kammwamba.

"The beauty, originality and obvious humour of his clay sculptures are amazing," wrote Stuart. I awaited the samples eagerly. This was his first buying trip; would he have proved his mettle?

As far as we knew, no-one was importing crafts from Malawi into the UK at the time, and when the samples arrived, it was clear why they hadn't attracted buyers. They were rough clay sculptures which looked as if they'd come out of a primary school art class. Stuart, however, was ecstatic.

"They're brilliant," he cried. "They're earthy, vibrant, creative…" I stopped him before he ran out of adjectives. Quick on the ball, he realised I was considering them from a more commercial perspective.

"They're also really well-priced, and completely different from anything else any other shops are selling," he continued.

"That's because no-one will want to buy them," I said. "They're awful."

However, I love to be proved wrong and I'm always keen to try something new. I agreed to give them a go. It was worthwhile; they weren't bestsellers, but they weren't a complete flop either. Unfortunately, after a year or two, they just stopped selling completely, and we weren't able to form the long-lasting relationship with Paul Kammwamba that we would have liked.

Stuart's trip continued. "When I joined Shared Earth, I didn't know

what I was letting myself in for," he remarked, after a whirlwind tour of jewellery workshops, wood-carving co-operatives and stone quarries in Kenya. Within a few days he had placed an order for five thousand Kisii soapstone carvings, weighing three tonnes. The fact that we had nowhere to store or even receive them had, apparently, not crossed his mind. However, the Yorkshire Evening Press obliged with a story, and to our delight a phone call followed which secured us our first warehouse in Lawrence Street, just outside York's city walls.

The Kisii stone was a hit from the start. Over the next year we placed four large orders, enabling the carvers' co-operative in Tabaka to install a clean water system for the village and to build a new primary school. Some of the designs were so successful that they were copied in China and Indonesia. Today you can buy them made in a number of countries; they have been copied in wood, resin and even glass.

Another order Stuart placed from Kenya, for hand-carved animals, jewellery and Akamba bags, holds the record for taking the most amount of time to reach us. Our agents reported that it was delayed due to "heavy rains" and "the holy month of Ramadhan when the producers don't engage themselves too much of activity." We later discovered that it had been sitting in a Nairobi flat whilst our agents had gone on safari.

Importing from Africa was a great step forward, and so was wholesaling our new range of recycled stationery. Both were a great help when we opened our next shop in October 1992. After the disaster in Wakefield, we had recovered and made a small profit in 1991. I was itching to expand again. Apart from Newcastle, where rents are very high, we had run out of large cities in the north of England, so I transferred my attention to the Midlands, where Birmingham was having a running battle as to whether it or Manchester was the UK's 'second city', after London.

I had looked at an empty shop on New Street the previous year, and it had looked promising. It had been winter, though, and the street was cold, damp and dirty. Pedestrians were few and far between, and seemed to be passing through, rather than showing any interest in shopping. The shop was boarded up and had been empty for years. Its rent was only

£19,000 per year, which was low for a large shop in a city centre. It was more than twice the size of our York shop, and half as big again as all our others.

"Do you think this would be a good site for a fair trade shop?" I asked a couple of people passing by.

"What's that?" they replied, in thick Brummie accents. We couldn't hear each other speak as endless buses and taxis revved up and down, belching fumes.

The café next door reported that trade was poor. I gave it up as a bad job.

Next year I was back. The shop was still empty, and had been bought by a property company, who had increased the asking rent to £35,000. It was summer, the street looked busier, and – this clinched it – plans to pedestrianise the street were under way. I was annoyed with myself for missing the opportunity to take the shop at the lower rent the year before, but decided to go ahead anyway. 87 New Street became our fifth and most successful shop to date, opening in October 1992.

Our next move was to be our last for many years. Our first floor at Goodramgate in York was now cramped to overflowing, with office and wholesale staff competing for space with the shop below, which had nowhere else to store its spare stock. We needed to move. In 1993 a site came on to the market on Minster Gates, at the junction of two of York's busiest tourist streets, Stonegate and Petergate. It was an excellent location. The shop was small but above it were two floors which were ideal for offices, and below it a basement.

Today, landfill sites are a problem – we are running out of space – but in terms of York's ancient history, they are a relatively new phenomenon. A few centuries ago, the basement of our Minster Gates shop was the ground floor. Years and years of rubbish and general detritus, thrown out of the windows or dumped in the street, have apparently raised the level of York's streets by several feet. The top of the basement windows are now at the level of the feet of the people passing by in the street above.

A few years previously, I had been a busker on York's streets. I was on Social Security at the time, struggling to keep my life together. Now, I employ over seventy staff. They will laugh when they discover where I used to busk. I rarely ventured from my favourite spot, which was

always busy with passing tourists. Where was it? Right outside the front door of our present shop. And it was, ironically, through busking that I saved up most of the money I needed to start a fair trade shop in the first place. If I had been told that I would be entering that same building, thirty years later, as the Managing Director of a business with a turnover of three million pounds, I would not have believed it.

In 1993, unusually, the landlords put the lease for the building up for auction. Our estate agent told me that a commercial rent for the property would be about £39,000 a year. It was less than I expected. We were all keen on the move, even the ever-cautious Jill Ashby, our first in-house accountant, who had joined us in May.

"Let's go for it!" I said. "It's a fantastic opportunity." Against all advice from our agents, I offered to pay a rental of £45,500, far more than the building's commercial value at the time. I reasoned that the office space alone was worth the extra amount, quite apart from the location. Almost all visitors to York go past the shop on their way to the Minster, Stonegate or the Shambles, another prime tourist street.

"Why not £45,000?" asked Jill.

"The extra £500 is to make sure we win, if someone else bids £45,000 as well as us," I explained. Ten years later, I discovered that another business had indeed offered a rental of £45,000.

We have not looked back. Today, the two upstairs floors are used to capacity. They include a small photo studio, a room for meetings, and offices for our accounts, buying, admin, wholesale and design teams – fifteen people in all. The basement is being renovated to accommodate further storage and office space, enabling us to take on more staff as we continue to expand.

In medieval times, the building used to be three houses, tall and narrow, and the shop is now divided into three sections. Before we moved in, it was a gift shop called Alpha Nova. I had looked inside many years previously, when I was selling recycled paper at a stall in the street. They had a great display in the front section, and a reasonable display in the middle section; but the back section was half empty. I remember being frustrated, even back then. Why couldn't they fill it with recycled stationery?

For a long time, environmental issues were not a high priority in the fair

trade movement, and for some organisations they still are not today. The emphasis was, and is, on reducing poverty through trade. Fortunately, people are becoming more aware of the links between the fair trade and green agendas. We all know that well-off countries are consuming more resources than the planet can cope with: but poverty is harmful to the environment, too. When people have no security, they have more children to look after them when they are old or unable to work. This leads to population growth and a greater demand for food and land. Many live in slums, shanty towns or villages without electricity; more trees are cut down for fuel. As global resources shrink, this is becoming a bigger and bigger problem.

It's a vicious circle. Increased consumption of resources contributes to global warming, which in turn increases poverty. There's no point in finding people jobs, fairly or unfairly paid, if their land is swept away by flooding. Cyclones, tsunamis and other extreme weather phenomena are becoming increasingly common; droughts are destroying crops, and with sea levels rising, some people in low-lying countries are already losing their homes.

In addition, the pressure on land and increasing oil prices are pushing up the cost of food. If people are suffering in Britain, where we only spend a small proportion of our income on food, how much more are people suffering in the Third World? A billion people are struggling to live on less than a dollar a day, and they spend more than half their income on food. For them, rising food prices may be catastrophic.

Fair trade and environmental concerns are inextricably linked. In the fair trade movement we need to become more aware of how global warming and other environmental problems are increasingly affecting the people we are trying to help. We need to make environmental issues a major priority, for instance by examining our operational policies and reducing our carbon emissions. We need to understand the issues better, campaign to raise awareness and work closely with the environmental movement.

Environmentalists need to be aware of the issues of poverty, the effect it has on the environment, and how trade can influence all of this. The depletion of the earth's resources has come about because of our demand for ever more products, sourced further and further away from where we

live. Trade is at the heart of this. There is an excellent opportunity today for environmentalists to work closer with the fair trade movement as it develops sustainable alternatives to normal commercial trade.

Andy Atkins, Director of Friends of the Earth, is another person who has extensive experience of development issues. He too believes that issues like the environment, justice and fair trade cannot be easily separated.

"The fair trade movement has been brilliant at bringing justice issues into the supermarkets and arousing the public conscience – that's been a massive breakthrough. Now the fair trade and environmental movements need to work and campaign together more. The linkages between what's right for the environment and what's fair for people are enormous! We have much to teach and learn from each other. Let's work together more!"

I totally agree.

9 The Whisky Security System

AGUNG ALIT, THE founder of Mitra Bali, is a kind of fair trade Indonesian hippy. His passion for fair trade is only equalled by his passion for rock music, and discussions about rural poverty never last long before he interrupts them with a burst of song, or an enquiry as to whether you like a particular band. When he visits Europe his first stop is the Hard Rock Café. His children are called Janis (without the Joplin) and Carlos Santana.

It was March 2008 and I was visiting one of his pet projects with one of our designers, Michelle Hughes. It's in a remote village called Desa Abuan where Mitra Bali has saved a family of woodcarvers from bankruptcy. In return for paying off their debts, Mitra Bali has the use of their land for ten years, and is planting it with Albesia trees (known locally as 'blalu.') Albesia is the main wood used in Bali to make crafts such as wind chimes and animal carvings. It's one of the fastest growing trees in the world, taking only seven to ten years to reach maturity. Some people in Bali talk about it as if it is a weed.

Nengeh Witiar and his family manage the plantation, and when the trees are harvested they will receive 70% of the income. From about 2010, they will have free timber to use for their carvings. In the meantime, they use the ground between the trees to plant cassava, potatoes and other vegetables. It's an excellent sustainable project, which has now expanded to include a further 27 families. Two thousand trees have been

planted; planting symbolically takes place on World Fair Trade Day each May.

Michelle and I entered the family compound, with Agung leading. Almost immediately he stopped.

"This is the toilet," he announced, pointing to our right. He was smiling proudly as if he were a guide showing tourists a noteworthy monument.

It was a small concrete shed with a corrugated iron roof. We had not asked for the toilet, but nodded politely. An outside toilet is the norm in Bali, where most houses consist of several separate one-room buildings, each with a different function: one for eating, one for receiving guests, one for sleeping and so on. As the Balinese are highly religious, there is also a family temple, often intricately decorated, outside which offerings are placed every morning. These family compounds often contain twenty or thirty people, including brothers, sisters and their families as well as grandparents and children.

"This is the kitchen," continued Agung, breaking out into song, "*buffalo soldiers, da-di-da, da-di-da* – it's good, isn't it. But the toilet is really excellent. Very good, very clean."

"Is there something special about the toilet?" Michelle asked, wondering why Agung was so keen to bring it to our attention.

"Oh yes," he replied. "There certainly is." His eyes shone with pride and his long hair gleamed in the sun. "We helped to build it. The family is very poor, you know. Very poor. *You* helped to build it – with your orders. You must pass on our thanks to your customers. Smile! Rock and roll!"

Agung's staff love him, not least because he gets drunk with them and has a great sense of humour. As we ate lunch he shared some of his less outrageous stories.

"We were having a workshop on finance for our staff and producers," he said, "and we arranged for a European consultant to come over and lead it. As you know, this is one of the things we try to do in fair trade – to make people more self-reliant by training them and improving their skills. Anyway, this guy hadn't been to Bali before.

"I met him at the airport," he went on, "picked up his bags, you know, carried them to the car. He thought I was the driver. I didn't contradict

him, why should I? I just pointed out tourist sights to him like all good drivers do – 'this is Kuta', 'that's the president's palace', that sort of thing. At the hotel he thanked me and told me I'd been very helpful. 'No problem,' I said.

"Next day he arrived at our office for the workshop and I heard him talking to Rah Aji, our Assistant Director. Aji's an elite kind of person, suit and tie, very smart, you know what I mean? They were getting on very well together. Then he nodded in my direction.

"'Who's your driver?' he said. 'He was very helpful last night. You've got a good member of staff there.' Aji couldn't work out what he was talking about. Then he realised.

"'You mean the guy with the ponytail?' he said. 'That's Agung, our founder and Managing Director.'"

Agung roared with laughter. His stories aren't just at the expense of his buyers, however. You've got to watch out, whoever you are.

"I took one of our woodcarvers to a trade show in Hong Kong last year," he remembered. "He was very naïve – he'd never been abroad before, hadn't seen western toilets at all, you know what I mean? I took him into one of those urinals where they flush automatically, you know? It was really posh – it even had a fly printed on it, showing where you're supposed to aim.

"He was banging away at the thing, trying to get it to flush and not knowing what to do. Getting very embarrassed. I was trying to stop laughing.

"In the end he gave up and started to walk off. And then it suddenly started flushing. He jumped up in the air, he was so startled! He didn't know what was going on."

Agung burst out laughing again. With his light-hearted attitude to life, he's not just good at telling stories, he's also excellent at charming the ladies. He recalled with affection his visit to Shared Earth a few years previously.

"I think you must be very good at recruitment, Jeremy," he told me, as we walked to the local pub with some of our staff at the end of the day. I was flattered, and smiled.

"Your staff are very friendly," he continued, and then went on, "very beautiful – I like. Your designers – wahey! When can I come back to see you again?"

Shared Earth helped to get Mitra Bali going in 1992. Our buyer, Stuart Browning, had spent ten days on the Indonesian mainland and on Java, where he placed a few small orders. He arrived in Bali in January, keen to investigate the possibility of ordering direct from producers there; at the time you could only buy fair trade Balinese crafts from Jakarta. He trudged along in the blazing heat. He was wearing a smart shirt and carefully ironed trousers. He knew that first impressions are important when you meet a new supplier.

Agung sauntered out to greet him, dressed in a T-shirt and surfing shorts.

"Why so formal?" he asked, laughing. "You think I'm some kind of businessman or something?"

He had brought his fiancé, Hanni, with him. She had a good job at the local bank, and along with it the use of an air-conditioned car, a luxury which Stuart, in his over-dressed state, appreciated as they travelled round Bali visiting producers. With her good looks, smart dress and fancy car, Hanni had already proved very useful to Agung.

"When I started, I went to see some producers to tell them about fair trade and how they could benefit from it. But they thought I was some kind of weird hippy. Maybe my hair was too long. So I got Hanni to take me to them again in her posh car. She always dresses smartly, too. 'Hanni's an important buyer,' I told them. 'She's an agent for some large companies in Europe and America. They could be placing some big orders.'" He laughed at the memory. "Then they started taking me seriously."

People think of Bali as an island of great beauty, which is true. Many tourists think it's a paradise, but appearances can be deceptive. Many of the hotels and restaurants are owned by politicians and army generals in Jakarta, so the profits from tourism don't all stay on the island. There's a lot of hidden poverty, and in some of the rural areas some people are still struggling to afford the basics of an adequate diet.

The extended family – grandparents, parents and children all living together, often with aunts and uncles and their children, too – is the norm in Bali, and crafts can be a useful form of additional income for the family as a whole. If the crops fail, there's still some money coming in.

Often the craftsmen and women group together to specialise in different styles and types of product. Stuart was taken on a guided tour of the 'duck village', the 'wooden fruit village', the 'frog village', the 'horse village' and the 'dolphin village.' He was amazed by the sheer variety and skill he saw. One style of carving is called 'antique.' In one workshop, he wrote, "about 25 people, both men and women, were carving wood, then making it look old, then painting it, then making the painting look old. The finished product was superb."

Agung had previously worked with Pekerti, a fair trade association in Jakarta, but this involved the clumsy and expensive operation of shipping orders from Bali to Jakarta, before exporting them abroad. Agung wanted to set up an organisation to export directly from Bali, but was worried about whether it would work. Stuart, enthused by all he had seen, had no doubt that Agung could manage to do it successfully.

"Go for it!" he told him, aware that his confidence needed bolstering.

"If I do, will *you* order from us?" Agung asked. Stuart immediately promised to do so. It wasn't long before box after box of woodcarvings was arriving in our shops – dolphins, banana trees, frog boxes and a host of other products, each made by the village which specialised in that particular craft. It wasn't long before Mitra Bali was our largest supplier.

My desire to import crafts directly from abroad increased further in May 1995, when I travelled to the biennial conference of IFAT, the International Fair Trade Association. When it was founded in 1989, IFAT's members were mostly from developed nations – the importers and sellers of fair trade products – but by 1995 it had grown to 87 members, almost a half of them from producer nations. Today it has over 300 members, two-thirds of them producers, and has changed its name the World Fair Trade Organisation (WFTO). The majority are involved in craft production, although food producers are well represented, too. 1995 was the biggest conference yet. Clearly IFAT – and fair trade – was growing.

That conference in 1995 was my first. It was held in Pennsylvania,

USA, and was an eye-opening event. I realised for the first time how desperate producers were for orders.

"You have a great catalogue," said a delegate from Sri Lanka, "and some brilliant designs. Some of Judy Byford's animal designs are fantastic, and it's great that you're getting them into mainstream shops. But they're all cards and stationery, made in the UK. Why don't you put some of them on to crafts, so we can get fair trade products into the mainstream too? I'm sure we can do things like this in Sri Lanka."

I was starting to get excited. I had always felt a bit jealous of Stuart, travelling to Bali, Kenya and other exotic countries. I had sent our York shop manager with him to Africa and I had even sent our Leeds shop manager, Jayne, with him to India. Stuart had since moved on: surely it was my turn to do some travelling? There were several potential fair trade suppliers in Sri Lanka. What's more, Sri Lanka wasn't far from Mumbai in India, where Asha Handicrafts were making T-shirts for us. Their manager, Lucas Caldeira, was at the conference and he too encouraged me to visit. It would be my first overseas trip since starting Shared Earth almost ten years earlier.

I hadn't been to India for fifteen years, and it was twenty-three years since I'd been there as an impoverished student on the hippy trail, discovering the world. I was desperately excited. I would be seeing India in a totally new light. If I could place orders, it would be a wonderful opportunity to repay some of the hospitality I had received there so many years ago. My first stop was Mumbai.

"I don't have a card – I'm saving the environment," said Lucas, as I arrived in Asha's office. That's a good line, I thought, must remember that one.

Asha (which means 'hope') is a Christian organisation which acts on behalf of producer groups across India, helping them to develop successful, competitive businesses. It educates them about fair trade principles, helps them to improve, and monitors their performance on behalf of buyers and customers. Like many of our suppliers, it checks quality before shipping, takes care of packing, customs and freight, and deals with all the invoicing. It also collates orders, so we don't have to order from each producer group separately.

Lucas was delighted that I was interested in buying more from Asha.

Previously, Asha had sourced cotton T-shirts for us, which had then been printed in the UK with Judy's animal designs. It was not the perfect solution. One of the problems of world trade is that the poorer countries end up supplying the raw materials, and the wealthy countries turn them into the finished product – and make most of the profit. The poor countries may not have the machinery or the infrastructure to manufacture, and are often restricted by quotas. The aim of these is to protect our industries, and it makes a mockery of 'free trade.' We tell developing countries we want to export our soft drinks, cars and technology to them – but we don't want them to export processed foods or clothing to us.

In the case of T-shirts, Asha couldn't find a printer at that time that could provide good quality colour printing on cloth. We ended up having to print them in Manchester, but there is an irony. It was the cotton mills in Britain that decimated the Indian handloom industry. This was the issue which inspired Gandhi to turn to the spinning wheel and weave his own clothes. Now Shared Earth is importing fair trade cotton from India, and selling it in fair trade shops in Britain.

But now I was back in India, offering contemporary designs; I wanted to explore the possibility of using our Animal Magic designs on crafts. In India, I thought, papier maché boxes would be a great medium for Judy's designs. They were made from waste paper over a thousand miles away in Kashmir. I loved the traditional paintings of birds and flowers on their lids, but I also knew they'd been around a long time, and customers had become tired of them.

In the early days of fair trade, however, buyers were desperately afraid of upsetting producers by changing their traditional designs. "In fact, we tried all kinds of ways of selling products we should never have bought in the first place!" Richard Adams commented to me recently.

"What would the producers think about painting Judy's frogs and cats and penguins, instead of peacocks and flowers?" I asked Lucas. "They're a totally different style, completely outside their tradition. Would they be offended?"

"They'll still be using their skills," he replied, "even if they're not painting the traditional designs. There's no point in going on with the old designs if no-one wants them. Producing boxes for you will provide them with work, and that's what they need – employment."

Asha's papier maché boxes were an example of how waste paper can be turned into an exquisite, artistic product. They would not have been out of place in the most fashionable art gallery gift shop. I ordered samples, and when they arrived a few weeks later I was delighted with them. The skill of the Kashmiri craftsmen was superb; Judy's designs had been reproduced exactly as we wanted. We placed an order straight away.

From Mumbai I flew to Colombo in Sri Lanka, where I was met by Modestus Karunaratne from Gospel House Handicrafts. A lot of people in Sri Lanka have long and complicated names, I discovered. Modestus drove me to a small hotel on the coast where I could step out from my room straight on to the beach. I opened the door, and walked onto the hot sand. Immediately, I was accosted by a man wearing shorts and a colourful shirt.

"You want hash?" he said. "Very cheap, good price."

"No thanks," I said, "I don't smoke." He followed me along the beach.

"You want girl?" he continued. "I get you – no problem."

I declined again, but he was still following me.

"You want boy?" he went on. Giving up did not come easily to him.

"No!" I said, stopping and staring him in the eye. "No! I don't want anything!" Eventually he got the point.

Walking away from the sea and into the nearby village, it was different. People stopped me in the street to practise their English and within minutes, a pretty young girl of about twenty had invited me into her house to meet her sisters and mother. They sat me at the table, brought out tea and snacks, and asked me whether I liked Sri Lanka, and what I was doing there. Soon they were taking it in turn to tell me their plans for the future, until eventually I left, feeling I could not have had a warmer welcome to the country.

Fair trade is about more than just buying and selling products. It brings people from different nations and cultures together, creating trust, friendship and understanding. It helps you to see people as people, not as

ideas or statistics. You begin to see that we really are part of one world. You could almost say that it helps to promote peace in the world.

Modestus picked me up the next day to show me around. Gospel House Handicrafts was founded by Modestus' father, who was a radio technician and a missionary, and so the family house became known as Gospel House.

"It was the seventies," explained Modestus. "Unemployment was 23% and my father was keen not just to preach the gospel but to help young people. He was making record-players, and then he got an order from a big company to make wooden boxes to pack apples. This allowed him to give work to about fifty young people. But when the job was completed, they were all out of work again. He was trying to think what he could do about this.

"Then another missionary who was leaving the country gave him his old washing machine. He was very skilled with his hands, and he took it apart and used the components to make a wood-working lathe. It's still working today, thirty years later! He cut out an old bed-frame to use as a base for the lathe and started making samples – egg-cups, saucers and things like that.

"To get things going, a local missionary sent a letter to a Tearcraft missionary he knew in England, asking if they could help him market the products. That was his big break. They put him in touch with Richard Adams, who came to see him. This was back in 1977.

"When Richard arrived my father was totally broke. He didn't have enough money to collect him from the airport. My mother had to pawn her wedding ring to pay for a taxi. Richard of course wasn't aware of this, but when he saw the lathe he was really impressed and placed a large order. He agreed to pay 50% in advance – otherwise my father wouldn't have been able to afford the raw materials to make the order.

"The first order was made in the open, under the banana trees that grew around it. In 1979 Tearcraft gave my father some money to relocate to Madampe, his birthplace, which is where we are now.

"I joined the business in 1981 when I was eighteen; my father was sick at the time. He died in 1983, and my mother took over. She retired in 1990, and since then my brother Shiran and I have been running the business together."

It was an inspiring story. I liked the products too, especially some 3D jigsaws for young children – dinosaurs, dolphins and other animals – which I ordered straight away. It was a great little workshop, providing employment and training for about 35 youths from the Colombo slums. I was fascinated to watch as a brightly-painted lorry arrived and disgorged a cargo of wooden planks, the raw material of the jigsaws. I wondered if some of that wood would be in our shops in a few months' time.

Next stop was a very different organisation with the name of Lanka Jathika Sarvodaya Shramadana Sangamaya. I could just see one of our sales assistants writing it down for a customer, and the queues building up while she tried to get the spelling right. After all these long names it was a relief when their Export Manager, a friendly Sri Lankan with missing front teeth, introduced himself. "Hello, hello," he said, shaking my hand enthusiastically. "My name's Paul."

Sarvodaya (for short) – which means 'universal uplift' or 'progress for all' – works in villages around the island, alleviating poverty and working for peace. It's a Buddhist organisation and is also inspired by Gandhian ideals. I was surprised to see a copy of a biography of Buddha, *The Light of Asia*, on Sarvodaya's bookstall. It was written by my great, great grandfather, Sir Edwin Arnold, and was a Victorian bestseller, but I assumed everyone had forgotten about it. Arnold's writing influenced Gandhi, and they met when Gandhi was a law student in England. Gandhi was the President and Arnold was the Secretary of the newly-formed Vegetarian Society. It was inspiring for me to find this personal connection.

My final visit was to another very different organisation, Golden Palm, which was founded by Ravi Jayawardena to provide employment in the rural areas of Sri Lanka. He asked me for a meal at his house, which turned out to be a mansion, with servants on call everywhere.

The meal was very different from the one I had just had at Sarvodaya, where we squatted on the floor for lunch. I had heard (rightly or wrongly) that Ravi was a member of the former Royal Family of Ceylon, and we sat at a table which would not have gone amiss at a sale at Christie's.

Ravi was one of the first people to become involved in fair trade in Asia. In the early days, he told me, fair trade was more talk than action.

"It took ages to take decisions," he recalled. "Buyers in Europe would sit around discussing things over and over again, losing market opportunities as they did so. There was a joke at the time – 'How many people do you need to replace a light-bulb in a fair trade organisation?' Answer: 'Five – four to talk about it and one to do it!' We've become more professional now," he added.

Golden Palm's aim is to create job opportunities in rural areas of Sri Lanka and, when I visited him, Ravi had just built a large production centre where two hundred people were making wooden items for the toy market in Europe and America. The profits are re-invested with producers in the form of tools, machinery and other facilities that help create better working conditions and more job opportunities.

In 1999, the centre was hit by a stroke of lightning and almost completely destroyed. Worse still, a clause in the small print of their contract enabled their insurance companies to avoid paying any recompensation. Ravi was devastated; but people rallied round.

"At the IFAT conference in Milan that year the director, Carol Wills, said straight away, 'Ravi, we are giving you a scholarship and refunding your conference fees.' More than half the delegates came and hugged me or sympathised. The solidarity was unbelievable. Word went round so quickly, and some buyers immediately promised assistance – over-the-counter commitments of $2,000, $10,000 – many more came in later. I didn't even have to ask. That's what fair trade is about – you wouldn't get that kind of comradeship in any other trade organisation."

Unfortunately, whilst I liked Golden Palm's products, they were geared more to the traditional toy market than to a gift shop like Shared Earth and I never placed an order. But I still see Ravi occasionally. Last time I saw him he gave me a useful tip for my travels, based on his own.

"I was in Kenya on safari with my wife," he said, "and we were staying in a chalet at the Mount Kenya Safari Club. It was very posh – jacket and tie strictly required – and we'd gone for a drink at lunchtime. I'd left my new video camera and a bottle of Black Label whisky in my room in one of my bags.

"When we got back after lunch the bag was missing! There were

muddy footprints all over the floor and the toilet window was broken. I ran to reception and screamed at everyone, 'I've been robbed! My camera's missing!' The chef, the security guards, the ground boys, everyone gathered round, and I berated the resident manager for not having a better security system.

"'Don't worry,' he said, 'we'll do all we can to get it back.' And two hours later, one of the security guards indeed came back with the bag. The camera was there, thank goodness. But the Black Label was almost finished.

"The robbers had also taken some of my clothes, but they were too big, so they'd thrown them on the ground, which showed which way they'd gone. They'd run off into the jungle. But they couldn't resist the whisky. There were two of them and they'd just drunk and drunk and drunk. Their stomachs were empty and they'd gulped it down, neat. It wasn't hard to apprehend them – the guard found them lying on the ground, completely sozzled.

"The moral of this story," Ravi added, "is that you should always take a bottle of whisky with you when you travel abroad."

We never ordered from Sarvodaya or Golden Palm. They tried to copy Judy Byford's designs but couldn't reproduce her style. We didn't want Sri Lankan hippos and elephants; we wanted Judy's. It's one of the problems of fair trade. As a buyer you meet some wonderful people, often running excellent projects, which have a big impact on the people at the bottom of society – the unemployed, the disabled, ethnic minorities, disadvantaged women and so on – and you really want to support them, but you can't buy from everyone. You have to turn people down.

Sometimes the price is too high. People generally believe that fair trade products are more expensive than normal ones. Whilst this is mostly true for food, it doesn't always follow for handicrafts. The difference between 'fair' and 'unfair' may mean only a small increase in the price the producer receives – $1.20 instead of $1, for instance – and the retail price may not be affected. If they like the product, many customers will still buy it whether it's £4.99, £5.99 or even £6.99. We were made

aware of this at Shared Earth when a customer told us our prices for jewellery were well below those of the high street chains. We realised what fantastic margins they must be making – and how easy it could be, financially, for them to switch to fair trade, with all the benefits that would have for producers abroad.

However, sometimes the price you're quoted really is too high, and unless you can change the design, use fewer raw materials or reduce production costs, you have to turn the product down. Commercial companies will negotiate to get the cheapest price possible, and it's always the producer who loses out most. In fair trade, we have a principle of accepting the quoted price, but we also have a duty to help our producers develop their expertise and learn about the markets in which their products are being sold. To do this, we sometimes tell them if a price is too high, and what it should be to make the product competitive. It's a dilemma, because they may then reduce the price just to obtain an order, and we don't want to exploit them.

In other cases, there's a wonderful producer group whose members are on the breadline, and you know their families will be going without food if they don't get orders. But the quality of their products is poor. There aren't any giraffes in Sri Lanka so when you receive a sample which looks like a camel with spots on, you can either laugh or you can despair. Especially if the paint is uneven and the wood cracks because it hasn't been dried properly. You can't order it, however much you want to support the producers. All you can do is try to help them to develop their skills.

In the case of Sarvodaya and Golden Palm, their products weren't right for our market, and they couldn't adapt their style to what we wanted. At Gospel House, however, a talented artist called Gerry Fernando, who was skilled in papier maché, copied Judy's designs successfully onto fridge magnets, and we sold these for several years.

We were also soon placing regular orders for Gospel House's 3D animal jigsaws. With the T-shirts and boxes from Asha, and the new woodcarvings from Bali, we were building up quite a menagerie. Our wholesale department was expanding fast. Baskets and wall-hangings were out of fashion; wildlife was in, and our Animal Magic range was top of the charts.

"We're selling a lot of animals today," commented one of our shop assistants to another. "It's great."

A customer overheard.

"I didn't know you sell livestock," she said. "How do you do that in a fair trade way?"

10 Boom And (Nearly) Bust

THE CRISIS IN Wakefield was a thing of the past. The recession was over, and our confidence was rising. We made our best profit ever in 1993, doubled it in 1994, and increased it by another 50% in 1995. It seemed as if the gods were back on our side, but fate is a fickle thing. It wasn't long before I made another error which nearly sank the business.

Things were on the up partly because of our move to Minster Gates in York and the success of our new Birmingham shop, but mainly because of our booming wholesale catalogue. Judy Byford's animal designs were sweeping the country. Orders flooded in from gift shops, museums, zoos, art galleries, corner shops, garden centres – almost any kind of shop, in fact, that sold cards or stationery.

We had expanded from greetings cards and gift-wrap into other types of stationery, too. "Our writing sets and notebooks are 100% post-consumer waste recycled paper!" we proclaimed, trumpeting our environmental credentials. The writing sets, which had animal designs on the envelopes, were especially popular, and we were now buying them in huge quantities. "We can beat the best with these great designs – and we're the only supplier in the UK selling such an excellent range of recycled paper!"

To cope with the extra demand we were renting space at a self-storage warehouse. It was the sort of place you leave your furniture when you go abroad, not meant for a growing wholesale business. It served us well

for a while, but our wholesale manager, Alison Jones, was becoming increasingly agitated.

"We're not the business we were when we started wholesaling," she told me. "Our sales have gone from a hundred thousand pounds to nearly four hundred in just two years. We've only got self-storage warehouse space and a tiny area for packing above our shop. And now you're buying boxes and jigsaws from India and Sri Lanka – they're a lot more bulky than cards, you know. We've got to look for a decent warehouse!"

I didn't tell her I was also planning to import a whole load of crafts from Bali, too. I was well aware of this problem, and gave her the go-ahead to look for a suitable warehouse.

Initially, however, she didn't have much luck. We looked at a dilapidated warehouse just off James Street, one of the streets scheduled for demolition by York Council in the 1970s. It had even been ignored by York Squatters' Association. James Street was demolished not long after, and the warehouse we were looking at should probably have been demolished too. It was in a frightful state.

Then, out of the blue, a warehouse in almost perfect condition came on the market. It had excellent office space, roller shutter doors, and a good security system. It was modern and it was the right size. Could we afford it?

"I reckon we'll need to increase our wholesale sales by 25%, just to break even," I told our senior managers. "We doubled our sales two years ago, and they were up 80% last year. What do you think?"

The answer seemed obvious. Increasing sales by a quarter seemed an easy target after the last two years of growth. While there's always a slight niggle of doubt in my mind when I embark on a new project, the arguments in favour were compelling. We were all optimistic, and Alison was pushing hard for us to move. Even if it doesn't work out, I reasoned, there must be any number of businesses which would take such an excellent warehouse off our hands.

And so, for the second time in my business career, I signed a lease which almost sent me into bankruptcy. Liz, who was a partner in Shared Earth, would have been made bankrupt too, and we would have lost our house, which was being used as security for our overdraft. We had two young children, and I have no idea how we would have coped.

✳❄✳

All went well to start with. The new offices were exciting. Instead of a tiny garret above our shop at Minster Gates, with a sloping floor and barely enough room for an extra chair, I had a new desk and a proper room to myself.

"I really feel like a Managing Director now," I told Liz. "Maybe I should have a PA to answer calls and arrange my appointments. And a secretary as well, perhaps."

But I knew appearances don't matter. I'd seen plenty of companies with flash offices and they weren't all making a profit. Success is about commitment, hard work and making the right decisions, not about smart sofas and posh receptionists.

Every Monday morning the first thing I looked at was the sales figures for the previous week – and it wasn't long before I started getting worried. 1995 had been a fantastic year, but in 1996 most fair trade shops started reporting a downturn in sales. Other gift shops were struggling as well. And they were our wholesale customers…

Meanwhile, our costs were going up. Alison, who was previously a teacher, had only limited commercial experience. She had taken on a large team of warehouse assistants and baggers, who packed cards and counted our writing paper and envelopes, and made them into sets. Most were in their late teens, and it was a great team – they were having a wonderful time. They were such nice people, too. Looking back, and comparing it with how we operate today, I can see we had far more people than we needed. The wage bill each month was going up, but I felt powerless to do anything about it. I didn't have any experience of warehouse management, and Alison insisted that we were only just coping with the people we had.

Sales in our five shops had increased the previous year. In 1996, however, they dropped by 8%. Wholesale sales went up, but only by a small amount – nowhere near the level we needed for the new warehouse to break even. September, when wholesale customers order for Christmas, was a disaster. It should have been our best month, and it was one of our worst.

What had happened? Our customers were clearly feeling the pinch and

were cutting back on orders. The novelty of Judy Byford's greetings cards was fading too, and none of the new artists we tried out to replace them had the same appeal. Combined with poor shop sales that Christmas, it put us in a dire position. The long quiet winter months – when gift shops always make a loss – were still ahead. It was a worrying prospect.

In the New Year we closed the warehouse down, sub-contracting our distribution to another company. There was no point in waiting and hoping for the best. We were back in crisis mode and needed to act fast. Our offices moved back to Minster Gates. We had been in the new warehouse for only eleven months.

Our new distribution company was in Suffolk, close to Felixstowe where most of our overseas orders arrive. They were on an old airfield, using abandoned aircraft hangars from World War II. The commission they charged us covered rent for storage, insurance, packing materials, admin and wages – and after a couple of months I realised how inefficiently we'd been running our own warehouse. We'd been spending as much on wages as they were charging us for everything.

When our shop closed in Wakefield, we'd been lucky; the landlord had let us out of the lease without any problems. Our warehouse landlords, however, wanted to screw us for as much as they could get. Yes, they would release us, they said. But we'd have to pay them £100,000 first. We couldn't afford this massive sum, so we just left the warehouse empty, hoping to find a new tenant.

"It's such a fantastic warehouse, someone's bound to take it off our hands before long," I said optimistically. "Just think how hard it was for us to find a warehouse like it when we were looking for one ourselves."

Month after month passed. A year went by, then two, then nearly three. Only a couple of people had even looked at it. More time passed, and still we kept hoping against hope that a tenant would turn up. It was like gambling; we were waiting for the lucky card.

"We could go on like this forever," I said. "It's like a millstone hanging round our necks. We've got to move on."

We stretched our overdraft to its limit and somehow, with a little help from our friends, managed to scrape together the funds to pay the landlords their £100,000. We'd paid over three years' rent on a warehouse

that we weren't even using, and spent a quarter of a million pounds on nothing.

Having paid off our landlords, we had to survive and recuperate. We had to watch every penny. Our overdraft never seemed to go down, and our bank manager's face grew longer and longer every time we saw him. Wages were frozen, and once again I did the rounds of our suppliers, begging for longer credit terms and larger discounts to help see us through. We closed our Bradford shop. Sales there had been going down each year, as shoppers increasingly went to Leeds instead, and now it was making a loss.

The threat of receivership – and personal bankruptcy – was never far away, but I was not going to throw in the towel without a fight. I had a plan.

First, of course, we had to reduce our costs. In the early nineties, when sales and profits were booming, costs didn't seem to matter. We'd measured our performance with detailed social and environmental audits. We'd run expensive training programmes using external consultants. We'd paid staff to produce thousands of product information leaflets. These were all luxuries and had to go.

Secondly, I wanted to change the whole direction of the business by expanding our overseas buying. The trips to India and Sri Lanka had whetted my appetite.

"Let's be positive!" I said to our staff. "This is going to be fantastic for our overseas partners. To make more profit we're going to cut out some of the middlemen and buy as much as we can from suppliers abroad. It'll be great for the environment, too! We'll import as much as possible by sea. Our new warehouse is right next door to Felixstowe, where all the containers arrive. Instead of being sent by lorry to York, over two hundred miles away, they'll only have to go to Stowmarket!"

"Yes, that's great, and it's all very well," said a sales assistant. "But are we going to lose our jobs?"

To improve our financial position, I knew that we had to import more. I also decided to break with traditional fair trade wisdom, and concentrate

on 'contemporary' as opposed to 'ethnic' design. I was impressed by the products coming from Bali. They were new and different, and the Balinese woodworkers seemed very skilful. Gerry Fernando, who made fridge magnets for us in Sri Lanka, was doing well. So were the papier maché artisans in India. But they could only make specific types of product. I decided to speak to Agung.

"We want to put Judy Byford's designs on pencils, wind-chimes and a whole host of other products," I told him. "We really want to expand our crafts. I've visited Sri Lanka and they're good at woodwork and painting, but they just don't seem to be able to copy Judy's designs accurately. Do you think you can do it in Bali?"

"Of course we can - no problem!" replied Agung. "Don't worry! Rock and roll!"

When the first samples arrived from Mitra Bali, we were delighted. They were perfect. Wind-chimes were a new craze, and there were lots on the market, but nothing which combined the ethnic chime idea with contemporary UK design. Initially we ordered a hundred of each design. Then two hundred. Then five. We couldn't get enough of them. Customers like London Zoo and a whole host of museums, garden centres, gift shops and wildlife centres had to queue up to get what they wanted. Cat shops ordered the cat designs; farm shops ordered the sheep; a gift shop in the Falkland Islands ordered hundreds of penguins.

Eventually we were ordering a thousand or more at a time. We went on to put Judy's designs on fridge magnets, keyrings, salad servers, bookends, picture frames, coat hangers, letter-openers, pencil boxes, even clocks. In 1999 we doubled the size of our wholesale catalogue, and more than half of it was crafts from Mitra Bali.

Gede Sukarsana, from a peasant family in the village of Basangambu, was one of the first producers to benefit. He was only twelve when he started learning the art of woodcarving from his father after school. When he left high school he decided to take it up full-time. With regular orders coming in from Shared Earth, he was able to build a spacious new workshop with plenty of ventilation, where woodcarvers and painters could earn half as much again as they could in agriculture. A skilled worker could earn three times as much.

Like many craftsmen and women in Bali, Gede Sukarsana sells his

crafts in a roadside shop in front of his workshop, and with the profits from fair trade he opened another shop next to a local temple. Today he also supplies gift shops in the tourist villages of Ubud and Kuta. This has enabled him to keep up his income despite a fall in orders from Shared Earth. Wind-chimes are no longer as fashionable as they used to be and, eventually, the appeal of Judy Byford's unique style faded. Ten years on we still sell some of those original elephants, dolphins and frogs that she designed, which is impressive when you consider how fast fashions change these days. However, we don't sell them in anything like the same quantities.

✭✦✮✭

One new range we started importing from Bali was completely different: 'antique' wooden cats.

I've never quite understood why gift shops sell ten times as many cats as they do dogs. We didn't even bother to commission a dog design from Judy. The fact is that cats keep selling and selling. We already had several cat products designed by Judy, but we knew we could sell many more. So when I saw these 'antique' cats, which were completely different in style, I was interested. However, they occasioned many arguments and strong feelings before I was allowed to order them. Some of our staff didn't like them at all. They sat on sofas, played golf, went fishing and flew in balloons. Some even wore clothes.

"They're terrible," said one member of staff. "Why do we have to make such beautiful animals fit in with our human viewpoint on life? It's total exploitation!"

"They're completely impractical," said another. "They're like the toucans we used to sell. The tall ones will fall over and get broken. Look! The ones on sofas come off! They'll get lost. It'll be a nightmare."

"They're awful!" said yet another. "They're so twee! They're just not the sort of thing we ought to sell – they don't fit in with our image at all."

"Well, I understand all your arguments," I responded. "In fact, I agree with many of them. But in the end, we're here to support fair trade and make a profit. We're paying rent on an empty warehouse and we've got

to increase our sales! And people love cats! I'm not saying I would or wouldn't put a cat playing golf on my mantelpiece. But if customers want them, and it helps the producers in Bali, we should sell them."

So we tried them out. They were an instant success, and still are today. Usually, products come and go; you have to replace them or customers get tired of them. But we're still selling some of those original cats on sofas ten years later, and they're still selling well. We stick blu-tac on their bums to stop them coming off their sofas.

Making these changes – cutting costs and buying more from overseas – was enough to see the business begin to turn around. We weren't safe yet, however. As Shared Earth struggled, how were other fair trade organisations coping?

It was a period of steady growth – and the start of huge change. Shops were opening regularly. Fair trade was becoming better known, and even commercial retailers were attracted, like Siesta in Canterbury, which had opened in 1984 but only become known for its fair trade credentials a decade later.

"To begin with," said Les Harper, who founded Siesta with his wife Chris, "I didn't feel comfortable using the words fair trade, because I thought it meant charity. Most of our wholesale customers were commercial gift shops, and our customers in Canterbury weren't fair trade supporters, they were people who came in off the street."

BAFTS – the British Association for Fair Trade Shops – was founded in 1995. The influence of more commercially-minded shops like Siesta and Shared Earth was to be an important influence in the way it developed. Meanwhile, the fair trade scene in Britain was changing fast. Handicrafts were giving way to food.

When fair trade took off in the eighties the development agencies weren't keen on selling food at all. They didn't like the idea of labourers in former colonies slaving away on the land, growing cash crops for us in our affluent societies.

Eventually, the World Development Movement put its name to a tea from Sri Lanka. This opened the door. Food was something people

bought again and again; it created jobs. As Richard Adams put it, "there was a limit to how much ethnic craft you could have in your house."

In 1991 Oxfam Trading, Traidcraft, TWIN Trading and Equal Exchange joined together to launch Cafédirect, a high quality coffee grown in Mexico and Costa Rica. It was a breakthrough – a quality product that anyone might buy. The following year, the Fairtrade Foundation was launched, and within two years the first Fairtrade Mark products had been launched – Cafédirect coffee, Clipper tea and Green and Black's Maya Gold chocolate. The stage was set for marketing Fairtrade food through the supermarkets. The first order, for Maya Gold chocolate, was placed by Sainsbury's in 1994. Interest from the supermarkets increased steadily – with the Co-op leading the way – and soon the supermarkets were registering their own fair trade brands.

As fair trade food became more easily available, some BAFTS stores suffered; the supermarkets were cheaper and easier to reach. At Shared Earth, we gave up selling food almost completely, with the exception of a selection of chocolate. I wanted to move into other areas. I was especially keen to expand our stationery range.

Our recycled paper had been a great success; but I wanted to sell fair trade paper too, which is almost always handmade. Handmade paper is one of the best sustainable products because it uses easily available materials which would have no other use – weeds, banana leaves, water hyacinth, cotton rags, waste paper – even elephant dung!

When people hear this for the first time they can't believe it. But it's true. Our first elephant dung paper came from Zambia, from a small village next to a wildlife park. The park was not well-known, and had very few visitors. Some of the villagers, struggling to make ends meet, had resorted to poaching for a living; as everyone knows, elephant tusks fetch a high price. Why not create proper employment, reduce the need for poaching, and use sustainable local materials all at the same time? It was a brilliant idea, based on the fact that elephant dung is full of fibre. In this respect it is similar to most of the other materials used to make paper.

A workshop was set up, and production started. Four months later our first order had passed through customs and was sitting on the shelves of our warehouse near Stowmarket. The first consignment arrived in York.

The cards were a rustic brown colour, and were painted with elephants, giraffes and other African animals. We sniffed cautiously and were pleasantly surprised. No stink, stench or even a pong at all!

It was a fantastic illustration of how employment can be created out of almost nothing, using easily renewable materials. The project was helping to reduce poverty and benefiting local wildlife too. There are many similar examples in fair trade today, where poor people in rural areas are starting to see the value of the resources around them. There could be many more. Fair traders, environmentalists and wildlife protectionists could be working together and creating all kinds of opportunities across the globe.

Equal Exchange, best known for its fair trade coffee, has an excellent project importing Brazil nuts from the rainforests of the Amazon. The nuts grow in pods, a bit like the segments of an orange, and the ripe pods fall to the ground in the rainy season (January to March). They are gathered by local people who move from their towns into the forest, where they live for several months collecting the harvest, and then transporting it either by boat or on their backs to the shelling and drying factories. It's a real alternative to clearing the forest for agriculture. Attempts to grow Brazil nuts in plantations have been unsuccessful because they are an inextricable part of the rainforest system. They rely on a specialised bee to pollinate them; there is even a species of frog which breeds only in the pools that collect inside the discarded pods. It's another example of how fair trade often goes hand in hand with environmental concerns – the classic 'win-win' solution.

"How about marketing our elephant dung cards with the slogan 'Shit More, Live Longer'?" suggested an imaginative shop assistant. "It's sure to attract people's attention."

I agreed that it would. The quantity of dung, however, was not the issue. What mattered was how many cards our customers were willing to buy. This is the problem with all such initiatives. There are thousands of peasant farmers in rural Africa who attempt to augment their income by making crafts. But how can they ensure that consumers continue to buy them once the initial spark of interest has faded? How can they make them different each year, yet alone keep up with modern fashion trends? With Brazil nuts, it's not a problem. Cards and handicrafts are different.

One of the most important services fair trade buyers provide to producer groups is showing them how to develop their products. At that time, we didn't have a design team at Shared Earth. I was doing it all myself. Even skilful designers find it hard to develop handmade cards with small producers. Imagination is key. You have to break away from the basic handmade paper, dye it in different colours, cut it in different shapes, experiment with different materials, and above all keep coming up with new and inspiring designs, year after year.

The market is also difficult. You're competing against printed cards – which are a lot cheaper. You're competing against big chains like Clinton Cards and Paperchase, and against large wholesalers who have enormous design resources behind them. You're also competing against the hundreds of new designers and entrepreneurs who set up in business in the UK each year, who are able to match the prices of fair trade producers abroad because they work from home, use cheap materials and don't expect huge rewards. They couldn't do this with embroidery, jewellery or woodcarving, but with paper they can. It's a real challenge.

I was determined to do all I could to meet this challenge! So I was delighted when I discovered a wonderful supplier in the Philippines, Salay Handmade Paper Inc (SHAPII), which adds dried flowers to its paper to create really imaginative designs.

Their correspondence whetted my appetite. When you receive a letter which begins 'Dear Sir Jeremy' and is signed by 'Purple Palamine,' how can you not be intrigued, especially if you're a middle-aged man susceptible to flattery? I resolved to visit Salay as soon as possible.

It was a fascinating journey into another culture. I arrived in Manila in July 1999. It was late in the evening and I was ravenous, so I stepped outside my hotel, hoping to discover an interesting Philippino restaurant. I was disappointed. The first restaurant I encountered was Kentucky Fried Chicken; the next was McDonald's, then Burger King. I knew there was a lot of American influence in the Philippines, but I didn't know the fast food chains had quite so much influence. It was not to be my night.

After a couple of days in Manila, I flew to the small southern island of Mindanao, arriving two hours later in Cagayan de Oro, a small city

heaving with traffic. The commonest vehicle was a sort of automated bicycle rickshaw, which carries passengers along fixed routes, and the jeepney, a long extended jeep with benches on either side at the back, which carries up to ten people. Each was painted in ornate colours and had its own name, such as *Pretty Boy*, *Wondrous Grace* and *Sealed Lips*.

Neil Rafisura from SHAPII met me and we walked round the huge local market together. Stall after stall sold nothing but rice, all kinds of different varieties, straight out of the sack. Then came a row of stalls with live chickens in tiny cages. A bare-chested man sharpened a knife ominously; I moved away quickly, assuming a chicken was about to be slaughtered.

"It's okay," said Neil. "That's his job – he makes a living from sharpening knives. You don't need to worry about blood spurting on you."

Meanwhile, it seemed as if everyone wanted to talk to me. Neil acted as interpreter.

"They don't see westerners very often here," he explained. "The men are saying 'Hey Joe!' and the women are asking if you're single. They all assume you're American."

From there it was a sixty mile journey to Salay, a large fishing village. It was a complete contrast to the Americanised, traffic-laden mayhem of Manila and the bustle of Cagayan de Oro. Manila had been close to gridlock for most of the day. Salay, once you got off the main road, was virtually traffic-free. I only saw one car the whole time I was there.

SHAPII was set up by Neil's mother Loreta, a nurse who was concerned about the number of young people emigrating to Cagayan de Oro because there was no work in Salay. SHAPII has generated so many jobs – over two hundred people work there now – that this flow to the city has largely been stemmed.

Loreta's husband, Reynaldo, is a doctor. He also earns money as a pig-breeder, sells fruit and vegetables in Salay's market, is SHAPII's DIY man (and a Director) and has become a much-liked local politician. As if having a doctor and a nurse isn't enough, there's a dentist on SHAPII's workforce and a midwife in the print-shop next door. Fair trade companies generally try to provide benefits to their workforce,

apart from just decent wages and working conditions. At SHAPII, everyone gets free medical and dental care, a rare benefit in a country like the Philippines.

I toured the factory with Loreta and was fascinated to watch the paper being made. Its basic ingredients are abaca fibre and a local weed, cogon grass, but all sorts of other things are added, such as banana bark, sawdust and pineapple leaves; one wonders if the local compost-heaps aren't losing out. To start with, everything is chopped up and thrown into large vats, where it's cooked for several hours at a very low temperature. The resultant mixture looks a bit like porridge, only even less edible. It's then pressed and poured into huge troughs where its consistency is tested and natural dyes are added if coloured paper is required.

Next, rectangular sieves are used to extract the wet paper sheets. These are then dried, either in the sunshine or on pipes, through which heat is 'recycled' from the cooking vats. Finally, the paper is cut to shape and – presto! – it's ready for conversion into whatever product is required.

So far, this process is similar to handmade paper-making in many countries. SHAPII's particular skill is in transforming its paper into greetings cards and stationery. Dried flowers and leaves are added to make intricate patterns, which can be adapted to whatever the customer wants.

The flowers come from local gardens; SHAPII gives seeds out to whoever wants them. When I visited Salay, the whole of the village was seething with colour, with bushes all over the place covered with tiny flowers in a variety of colours. In the tropical climate, they bloom throughout the year. They include not just well-known flowers like daisies and marigolds but others with intriguing names like Billy Goal Weed, Bachelor's Button and Hoary Stock.

SHAPII has been recognised by the Philippines' government as a model in creating rural employment without large investment. Its production unit is airy, well-lit and uncongested, and as well as providing medical care, it runs 'livelihood groups' in skills such as soap-making, basket-weaving and mushroom-growing. It provides English classes at lunch-times, and interest-free loans to help its workforce improve their sanitary facilities at home, access the electricity supply and so on. Employees are also able to become share-holders, and there are scholarships for promising young teenagers to help them through college.

All this amounts to a fantastic boost for the whole village. By discouraging young people from moving to Cagayan de Oro, SHAPII helps both to reduce urban sprawl and to strengthen family and community life in Salay. I had no hesitation about placing large orders, and they later proved a real help in pulling Shared Earth out of its financial difficulties.

I became aware of the problems of rural poverty in the Philippines on my first night in Salay, at Loreta's house. There were five doctors round the table as we ate: Loreta's husband, three other doctors from the Philippines, and one from Germany. With five doctors and two nurses (Loreta's daughter is also a nurse) I would have been well provided for if I'd fallen ill; they'd have been fighting over each other to see who could cure me first.

"We're on a mission into the interior for six weeks," the German doctor told me. "It's very mountainous and people live hard and simple lives – there's no electricity, running water or anything like that. People have to struggle to get food on the table. It's a pretty basic existence and women have a lot of children – the average is about ten. I met one woman today who had twenty-one children! A lot of people only eat meat about once a month. But I've been pleasantly surprised, we've only found six or seven cases of severe malnutrition altogether."

Loreta and her family, who are well-off by comparison, open their doors to anyone who wants free food at religious festivals.

"Last time we roasted two pigs," said Neil. "It's the national dish. We had queues of people from the mountains coming down to eat, but we had to 'mark' them. We discovered some people were coming back and putting the food in boxes to take away."

I thought of Dr Ashley, my doctor in England, whose life is very different from that of Dr Rafisura or these German doctors. I often see him before I go abroad on a buying trip. We make the most of our time together; time in the NHS is short. Sometimes, though, he has more questions for me than I have for him.

"Where do you think I should go on holiday next year?" he asked me once. "I know you travel a lot with your business." I did my best to make useful suggestions.

On another occasion it was presents. "What do you think I should buy

my wife for her birthday, Jeremy?" he asked. "You know a lot about gifts, don't you? They're fairly traded too, I believe, aren't they? What can you recommend?"

His own advice is not always related to medical matters. I recently took my two sons and my nephew on a fair trade/safari tour of Kenya and Tanzania. I was hoping to teach them about fair trade, and give them an idea about what it's like to live in a developing country, as well as the excitement of seeing some of Africa's wildlife. I asked Dr Ashley about inoculations.

"Oh, just see the practice nurses," he said, "they see to all of that nowadays."

He paused for a second. "You'll have to get up early in the morning, you know," he continued, looking at me enquiringly as if that would be quite a challenge.

"Oh, that's ok," I replied, "I normally get up early these days."

"I mean *very* early," he went on. "You should really get up at the crack of dawn."

This was a bit puzzling. Did inoculations only work if administered early in the day? Or was I just being given some practical advice so I could avoid a long queue?

He smiled and tried to explain. "They'll be gone by mid-morning," he said. "You'll miss them if you leave it too late." He sounded really concerned.

He realised he still wasn't getting through. I was looking more at a loss than ever.

"I'm talking about the animals," he explained. I think the word 'dumbhead' also came out, but I don't want to get him into trouble.

11 The Wood City Of Saharanpur

WE DID INDEED see the animals in Kenya and Tanzania. We saw lions, antelopes, hippos, giraffes and elephants. We even thought we saw a rhino, though after twenty minutes peering at it through binoculars, we decided it was probably a rock. We spent three days climbing Mount Kenya, and as the trip progressed, learned more about the links between conservation and tourism, and the problems of income generation in large parts of rural Africa, where extreme poverty is widespread.

Why are people in rural areas so badly affected? The migration to the cities seems never-ending. What is this pressure to move to an urban life when for most people it seems to cause more suffering? The long hours working on the land must be exhausting and the remuneration must seem pitiful when they catch a glimpse of the leisure-filled lifestyle of the rich. Are they lured by the prospect of wealth, owning a car perhaps, or 'making it to the big time'? Are they worried about the risks of drought, floods or the natural disasters which may ruin their crops and lead to starvation? Are they desperate because they never know what price they'll get in the market for their crops, and whether they'll earn enough to feed their families? The answer is probably a mixture of all these things.

I met a wizened old man on the path to a country market, leading a goat on a piece of string. I asked him how much he had paid for it. He looked surprised – why was I asking? Yet the need to make a living was paramount. He sensed an opportunity.

"It's an excellent animal," he said. "Look…" He pointed out its sturdy legs, healthy skin and clear eyes. "For you, only 9,000 shillings."

I tried to explain that I was from England, and that it would be hard to get it on the airplane, let alone through customs. He walked away disappointed but hardly surprised.

Arriving at the market the first thing I saw was a group of stalls selling hot meals, and a collection of shacks with benches arranged in a square, full of men and as many women, drinking out of huge mugs that looked as if they would hold at least two pints.

"Hey, brother!" called an elderly lady. "You want to try?"

It was a local brew, a kind of beer I think, though it looked more like a cross between dirty dishwater and the yellow froth you sometimes see polluting rivers. I understood it was very bitter and extremely potent. I'm afraid I chickened out and declined the lady's kind offer.

I saw at the market how much village life must have changed in recent years. The stalls – mostly strips of tarpaulin laid on the ground – were covered in everything from food and clothing to household objects, farming implements and bicycles. Part of the field was filled with pens full of goats and cattle and there was an open area where they were sold by auction.

So far, I imagine the scene would have been a similar one twenty or thirty years ago. It was when I looked at the household goods and clothing that I sensed a big change. Not long ago, many of these products would have been made locally – if not in the immediate area, then at least within East Africa. But almost everything I saw here seemed to be made in the Far East. From clothes-pegs to buckets and from saucepans to knives, mass-manufactured plastic and metal, mostly from China, was everywhere. The clothing was also from the Far East, mostly cheap rejects, presumably sold at huge discounts to wholesalers in the capital.

The demand for hand-crafted items and traditional cloth – which not long ago were in common usage – was shrinking to an increasingly smaller group of people, largely old people and tourists, and there weren't any tourists in this area. The market was in a large field, with no access by car or lorry; everyone had either cycled or walked, sometimes for many miles, to get there. It was a stark contrast to the high-tech manufacture of most of the goods on sale. Villagers with traditional skills, who would

previously have supplemented their income from agriculture by making clothing, baskets and other household products, could no longer compete with these cheap imports. It was another reason to move to the city.

I bought a pair of trainers, inscribed with the words 'Bao Da' and an imitation Nike logo, from a woman who looked as if she was desperate for a sale. She was obviously very poor, and I wanted to help; but I felt guilty at the same time. I didn't want to support this way of doing things.

⊀⊰⊁

You see the same kind of thing in India – a plethora of plastic, mass-produced household goods in the local (non-tourist) shops. But it's only one side of the story. The handicraft industry in India is thriving, and provides more jobs than any other sector, agriculture aside. Its diversity is astonishing. The textile industry alone is enormous, with over ten million hand-weavers producing goods for both domestic and export markets.

Many are produced in sweatshops where hours are long and wages are meagre; child labour is common. As we expanded our crafts, I was determined that Shared Earth should buy more from India – increasing work for the artisans, but avoiding exploitation at all costs.

When we finally paid off our warehouse landlord, we were only buying from one supplier there, Asha Handicrafts. At IFAT's 1997 conference in Ooty, a hill station in the south of India, I met several more potential suppliers, and two years later I consolidated some of these contacts at the next conference in Milan.

The Indian delegates and I had a mutual interest – food. Like many of them, I don't eat meat. At Ooty, the food had been outstanding, and I had been looking forward to Milan for weeks, anticipating a variety of mouth-watering pastas and delicious sauces.

The conference was held in an ancient monastery in the countryside. Donations to the Church were not what they used to be; the monastery had to take in visitors, such as ourselves, to pay its way. The monks, however, were still in charge. I sensed a certain asceticism; food was for eating, not for pleasure. When the first meal arrived, I was disappointed.

Meat, potato and veg. The next day was the same. Someone must have complained, because the following day we had a choice of potato or pasta. The contingent from India was getting upset. Next day it was meat, white rice and veg.

"Do you have a vegetarian option?" I asked.

"Well, yes," the monk in charge told me, "I'm sure we can give you some grated cheese instead of the meat. That shouldn't be a problem." My face obviously showed that I was hoping for more than this.

"I think we could cook you an egg or two as well, if you like."

An Indian delegate went into town to search for some spices, at least, to add some flavour to the potato/pasta/veg. It was not the best of conferences from a gastronomic point of view. Instead of discussing fair trade as we ate, we seemed to be talking about food all the time. However, meeting so many Indian delegates spurred me on to plan another visit to India. I wanted to see the producers first hand. There was the added attraction, of course, of excellent vegetarian food.

A few months later I was on the Transpennine Express train for Manchester. This time it wasn't to visit our shop on Piccadilly Gardens. I was heading for the airport – and New Delhi. The eight hour journey couldn't go fast enough, and my excitement mounted as I stepped off the plane and experienced again that distinctive tropical smell of India. Even more so as I travelled through the crowded streets to my hotel and saw once again the cows on the roads, the signs for the *Budding Blossoms Nursery* and the school for 'Conversasional English.' My hotel was as welcoming as ever. It was early evening and I was hungry. I took an auto-rickshaw – a kind of scooter with three wheels and two seats behind the driver – to Dilli Haat.

Dilli Haat is a pedestrianised area in a suburb of New Delhi, which contains about two hundred craft stalls. Most are run by the craftsmen and women themselves, or their families, and the stalls change every two weeks, so there's always something new to find. All kinds of handicrafts are on offer – textiles, wood, stone, brass, paper, paintings, jewellery – you name it, there's a pretty strong chance it'll be there.

Sometimes the stalls are run by fair trade organisations, but most are small family businesses. They're a bit like the stalls you see at farmers' markets in Britain. Dilli Haat is a chance for them to avoid middlemen,

and sell direct to the public for a couple of weeks. They would love the advice on marketing, design and business management that producer groups like Mitra Bali and Asha Handicrafts can provide. What stops them, then, from joining the fair trade movement?

The answer is simple. The market for fair trade products is still not big enough. The more customers insist on fair trade, the more orders can be placed abroad, and the more work there will be for artisans – on fair trade terms.

Many producers sell only a small percentage of their work to fair trade – twenty or thirty percent, perhaps. The rest goes to normal commercial buyers, whose terms are far worse. They only pay when an order is completed, so the producers may have to borrow money at extortionate rates to buy the raw materials. They allow insufficient time for production. They may even cancel orders after they've been completed, leaving the artisan with no income and a pile of dead stock. "Sorry, that's your problem, not ours. Our customer changed their mind."

There are also permanent stalls at Dilli Haat, with tables and chairs scattered round them, selling meals and snacks. Each specialises in food from a different part of India. You can buy dhosas and coconut curries from the south, rotis and dhals from the north, even Chinese-style stir-fries from Arunachal Pradesh in the far north-east. The prices are cheap and when the food arrives, the dishes are piled high. One is sometimes enough for two or three meals, if you'd only known before ordering.

After an excellent meal of rice and cheese curry, I went to the toilet; the door was being mended, and a sign, 'We Apologise For Your Inconvenience,' had been tacked outside. It was January, in the middle of the Indian winter. In the daytime the weather is a bit like an English summer day, but the evenings are often chilly. The streets are full of people huddled around fires trying to keep warm, and you see policemen in greatcoats who look as if they've stepped straight out of Dr Zhivago. As I came out of the toilet, I shivered. I wasn't expecting weather like this in India. I needed something warm to wear.

Dilli Haat was the obvious place to look, and I soon found a stall selling handmade woollen jumpers, similar to those you see from Nepal or Peru. I agreed a price for one, and – at the last minute – decided I ought to try it on first. It was a good job I did. I could hardly get my head through the neck of the jumper.

I put my money back in my pocket and was about to leave; but the woman running the stall would have none of it. "Nahi, nahi!" she said – "No, no!" A flood of Hindi followed as she put her hands round my neck and started squeezing in and out.

For a minute I thought she was trying to strangle me. I tried to protest, but it was the end of a long day and my thought processes weren't working very fast. After a while, I realised she was telling me the jumper was too tight around my neck – which of course I already knew. She pointed at her wrist – she didn't have a watch but was obviously referring to one – and put ten fingers in the air. Then she waved a pair of knitting needles at me, smiling and nodding her head vigorously up and down.

I gathered from this that she could alter the jumper in ten minutes. I nodded and smiled myself – "acha, acha" – "good, good" – and started to walk away. This was not to her liking. Her right hand shot out and she beckoned significantly. Money please! She wasn't having me going away and not coming back. Ten minutes later I returned, to find the jumper had been altered; it fitted perfectly.

Can you imagine getting that kind of service in Britain? How many sales assistants can even use a knitting needle?? The time when tailors, watch-menders, blacksmiths and other tradesmen were around is long gone. We live in a throw-away society where if something breaks or wears, it's easier to buy a new one than to have it mended.

There were several people I wanted to meet in New Delhi, but I was especially keen to meet Padam Kapoor. Padam worked for the Indian government as a handicrafts specialist for thirty years, until in 1987, tired of bureaucracy, he left to become the Indian trade representative of Community Aid Abroad, the Australian branch of Oxfam. In 1993 he set up his own business, Aspiration, with CAA as his main customer.

An erudite, well-dressed businessman, on the surface Padam is as unlike Agung from Mitra Bali as you can imagine. But when you get to know them both, you discover they have a lot in common – an excellent sense of humour, for instance, a passion for the welfare of the craft people they deal with, and great courtesy towards their visitors.

They are both great story-tellers, too. Padam was keen to put me at my ease. The tea arrived on the table of his basement office and we talked about travelling to Jaipur, a great craft centre not far from New Delhi. He sipped his tea slowly. It reminded him of a journey he had made to Jaipur a few years previously.

"It was a hot day," he told me, "very hot in fact. So I stopped for a drink at a roadside café. I ordered tea. I can tell the difference between a good cup of tea and a bad one, you know, but – believe me – I had never tasted a cup of tea like this before. It was wonderful.

"I enjoyed it so much that I thought I'd have another one. So I got up to order it. I was trying to work out what was in it; I thought it must be some special blend of Indian spices. What was it that gave it that distinctive flavour that was making me feel so good?

"Suddenly I realised – it was flavoured with marijuana." He paused, then laughed. "I decided, as I was driving, it was probably better not to have a second cup."

Kantha, Padam's partner at Aspiration, is – like him – well past retirement age, but in other respects they are very different. Padam is tall and well-built. Kantha is tiny, but has lots of energy; she flits around like a bird. He reflects before he speaks, and does so slowly; she thinks on her feet, and talks quickly. They are both very generous, and Kantha is always praising people. She's quick-witted too, despite being in her seventies.

"You are speaking very good Hindi words today, Jeremy," she told me, smiling as if I was a star pupil.

"Thank you," I replied, "that's very kind of you." I had been trying to extend my Hindi vocabulary, so her remark was gratifying. When I thought about it, however, I couldn't remember having spoken anything in Hindi that morning. What was she talking about? I asked her what she was referring to.

"What did I say exactly, Kantha?"

"Yes, two and a half," she replied, as if this explained it all. I had been measuring the dimensions of some wooden boxes.

"But that's English," I said, even more puzzled than before. Kantha reflected briefly. It didn't put her off for long.

"Oh yes," she responded brightly, "you are right. We use many English words in our Hindi language today, you see."

One of the first products Aspiration sourced for Shared Earth was patchwork wall-hangings. These colourful hangings originated several centuries ago in Turkey, where woven cloth was put on the backs of camels and donkeys to protect them from the cold of the mountains. Nomadic tribes carried the tradition through Asia to Afghanistan and Pakistan, and eventually to India. With the introduction of needlework it was also used to make decorative outer garments for the nomads themselves.

During the 1971 India-Pakistan war, many skilled artisans migrated to Rajasthan in north-west India, bringing with them a huge collection of old pieces, which they sold to tourists. When these ran out they began to use pieces from old embroidered saris and other garments, adding them in patchwork fashion to a large backcloth. The tradition continues today. It's a good example of an eco-friendly/fair trade product – using recycled materials to create work for people who might otherwise be struggling.

With his knowledge of Indian crafts, Padam is capable of sourcing almost anything. Aspiration's speciality is wood, which comes from Saharanpur, a small town in Uttar Pradesh, about one hundred miles north of New Delhi, close to the border of the Punjab. It was to Saharanpur (the 'wood city of India') that Padam, Kantha and I headed, with Shared Earth's Spanish designer Itxaso, to visit some of the woodcarvers and their families.

Saharanpur's economy is rural based. Most of its food is grown locally; even in the centre of town many houses have cow-byres, and most families keep domestic animals such as goats, pigs and hens, which scrabble for food in the narrow streets outside their houses. Our journey was frequently held up by herds of sheep. At the time of our visit the sugar-cane harvest was being brought in, some by truck or bicycle, but mostly on carts drawn by bullocks or horses. The majority is processed with hand-operated extractors in various locations across the city.

It's desperately hot in summer, but in winter many poorer people succumb to death because the cold is so intense. There's not much greenery in the streets; there's just not enough room. There are, however,

countless shops either selling wood or processing it; craftsmen squat on the ground everywhere chopping it roughly into shape, carving delicate patterns, or using their traditional techniques to inlay thin brass wires to complete a design. The final stage of production, polishing, is carried out by the women. Machinery is minimal and most of the work is done sitting cross-legged on the floor.

Woodcarving in Saharanpur is geared around extended family groups: extra cousins, uncles and other relatives are brought in to help at busy times. The main family usually lives next to or behind their workshop, and the flat roofs (most houses only have one floor) are used to store the sheets of wood, which have to dry in the sun for at least six months before use. Piles of wood lie all around and the streets are full of bullock carts, lorries and bicycles carting it from place to place. There are more wood shops in the town than shops selling food, and sometimes it's hard to get inside them as they're crammed full with tables, boxes and ornaments packed into every nook and corner.

The main wood used for traditional woodcarving is shesham wood, which is grown in plantations to the north of Saharanpur. Some are owned by business people and some by Government Forest Officials, who manage the plantations and regulate the wood flow by felling only the oldest trees, or those that are diseased, and then planting new saplings. The chopped wood is sold in the market, usually by auction.

When we say that a wooden box is fair trade, we're referring to the conditions in which it's been carved – to everything that happens after the wooden logs have been bought by the artisan. There's a big question mark surrounding what happens before that. Who manages the trees? Who fells them? What kind of wages are they getting and how are they being treated? We just don't know. It's the same with a lot of fair trade products. When we buy silver or metal jewellery, for instance, we usually don't know how the silver and metal has been mined.

With cotton clothing and T-shirts, it's the other way round. Cotton with the Fairtrade Mark is now widely available and Marks and Spencer sells Fairtrade T-shirts at only £5 each. This causes confusion. The Fairtrade Mark applies to the growing of the cotton only; it may be milled in a commercial mill and the clothing may by dyed, cut and sewn together in a commercial workshop. But the staff on the shopfloor at M&S don't know the difference.

"You've got a sign saying this cotton is Fairtrade," I enquired at their superstore in York recently. "Does that mean the T-shirts are manufactured in a fair trade way too?"

"Well, they would have to be, wouldn't they?" replied the girl on their customer service counter. "Otherwise they wouldn't be called Fairtrade." Two other assistants stood next to her.

I explained the difference again so they knew exactly what I meant.

"That's what the label's for," said another girl, "so you know it's completely fair trade."

The story was the same at another branch I visited later. Although M&S stocks an excellent range of products with the Fairtrade Mark, it could do a better job at training its staff, I thought.

The sad fact is that quite a few fair trade products aren't perfect, whether it's at the raw material or the manufacturing stage; but we have to start somewhere. Fair trade is not just a technical process of ticking boxes – good wages: yes; decent conditions: yes – and so on. It involves adapting our principles and aspirations to different products, countries and circumstances, and recognising that none of us are perfect anyway. The main thing is that we constantly try to improve.

✳✦✳

Padam visits Saharanpur regularly, but its lanes and by-lanes are so narrow, and look so alike to an outsider, that even he can easily get lost in them. A guide was essential, and the morning after our arrival an artisan called Gulfam arrived at our hotel with another woodcarver on his scooter to show us around.

Most woodcarving families are Muslims; their designs go back several centuries to the glorious art of Persia, thousands of miles to the west. Gulfam is highly religious. His flowing shirt, skullcap and beard, coloured with bright red henna – and the stern look on his face – could have marked him out as a potential terrorist to a crowd in a frightened city in Britain. He approached us slowly, frowning, but suddenly a broad smile broke out across his dark face. "Namasté!" he said, "Hello, greetings. You are welcome to be here and I am honoured to show you around."

We were an unusual party. Itxaso and I, Padam and Kantha, Gulfam and his friend – two Christians, two Hindus, and two Muslims, all with our different skills, cultures and lifestyles, but all working together and benefiting from trade. We still work together today, and all of us – seller, exporter, craftsman – rely on one another to make a living from fair trade. It's not just about money, however. Because our aim is not to exploit, but to work in harmony for the good of all involved, we develop relationships which go beyond just trade. We begin to see each other as people, and to respect each other's differences. We smile, we share jokes. Suspicion, misunderstanding and prejudice between religions – even hatred – are common today. This affects politics and leads to human rights abuses, terrorism and wars. The aim of fair trade is not to deal with religious tension, but by bringing people together on the basis of mutual gain, it does help to reduce mistrust and tension and to create positive feelings and relationships. This aspect of fair trade is often overlooked.

In business, too, fair trade sets a different agenda. The top priority in conventional business is to maximise profit, and if this means other people or the planet suffer, well then, so be it. Competitors are viewed with mistrust; it's a dog-eat-dog world.

Attitudes, however, are changing. This is due in no small part to the achievements of the fair trade movement. We have mobilised the public on our side, and in the 1990s, conventional businesses started responding to consumer demand. We're now at the stage where some business leaders are not just following the fashion, they really believe it's right to trade more ethically.

Fair trade is not a charity. We want everyone in the trading chain, from producer to consumer, to benefit. We often refer to our suppliers as partners; we even work together with our competitors in the fair trade movement, sharing information, ideas and even product designs. We try to assist one another if problems arise, and this is not just a one way thing from 'rich' to 'poor' countries. When Shared Earth had to pay off its warehouse landlord, producers helped us by modifying our payment terms and allowing extra credit. This concern for one another helps to build up trading relationships that last for many years. Indeed, long term relationships are one of the aims of fair trade – to give producers security,

to allow them to plan a better future for themselves, their families and their communities.

As a movement that cares about people, what better advertisement could there be for fair trade than the example of Aspiration, Shared Earth and the woodcarvers of Saharanpur? Businesses run by people from three different religions, all working together with everyone benefiting, with the good of the people who need it most foremost in our minds?

Fair trade is certainly needed in Saharanpur. The houses most people live in are made of brick without cement, and the rooms are often dark and dingy. The electricity supply is intermittent; most people rely on candles at night. The woodcarvers have large families, but poverty and illiteracy are everywhere. Many boys work in woodcraft from an early age because their families need them to contribute to the family income.

Girls are usually married off very young and are subjected to household chores long before that. The women use traditional 'chulhas' to cook, with wood and wood-scrapings for fuel, and the air inside many homes is polluted by smoke, causing many lung-related illnesses. The municipal authorities don't seem to care; in the streets outside, vegetable waste and other rubbish lies around everywhere, and the unhygienic surroundings lead to an increase in flies, mosquitoes and infectious diseases.

Fair trade makes a difference. Gulfam, for instance, never went to school; his daily wages as a boy were needed to support his elderly parents and younger brothers. As an adult he came into contact with Aspiration, who helped him to set up on his own. He never looked back. He is now 27, and since Shared Earth started supplying Oxfam, his family has really benefited, as he explains:

My name is Gulfam – not at all educated can only write name in Hindi – an artisan of woodwork… I used to work on daily wages with other big producer units till 1997. Got married and had a son. I had to take care of my parents and younger brothers and it became difficult to manage…Since last two years I have been getting big orders from Oxfam through Aspiration and Shared Earth. With the earning from big order myself along with seven members of my unit have been able to provide more basic comforts to my family… My three children are studying in good school in Saharanpur. I am now being respected in

my community. This has been written original in Hindi by my elder son who is 12 years old and his name is Danish. God bless Oxfam and we keep on getting good orders!

An important aim of fair trade is to enable people to improve their living standards, so it's really gratifying when you visit someone who has moved from a slum to somewhere more permanent. I've seen this in Saharanpur, and I've seen it in Bali, where I've visited people who have built a new house as a result of our trade with them.

The most interesting house I've been to, however, was owned by a craft producer in Kolkata. He made a living by making mobiles from scraps of old textile materials.

I had already surprised him, as I surprise many people in India, by saying I don't drink tea. Indians are always hospitable, and they are not prepared for this. "But you are Englishman!" they exclaim. Like the Pakistani customs official who assumed all Englishmen were clean, when I travelled to India in 1972, most Indians assume the English live for their next cup of tea.

As I sipped a glass of water, I received a surprise myself. I suddenly became aware that I was sitting next to what looked like a tree trunk. Not lying on the floor, but coming up through it and continuing upwards through the ceiling. I felt the bark. Yes, it really did feel like a tree.

"Is this a tree?" I asked, somewhat hesitatingly. I didn't want everyone to laugh at me.

"Oh yes, that's our coconut tree," replied the producer nonchalantly. From the way he said it, you would have thought it was the most natural thing in the world to have a coconut tree growing in your living room.

To prove his point he took me up to the roof, which was used for cooking, growing plants in pots, hanging laundry to dry and so on. It was like a garden, with pots of herbs and vegetables – and the top of the coconut tree. I made a suitably admiring gesture, and a joke (which doubtless he had heard many times before) about not having to climb far to harvest his crop. The family, apparently, had built the house around the tree. It was a valuable resource which they didn't want to destroy.

12 Reject Our Goods!

"WE WANT YOU to reject our goods!" announced an African producer, pausing to achieve his effect. He was speaking from the floor at an IFAT conference and delegates from across the world were listening intently. What on earth was he talking about?

"You are all so generous, so nice to us," he continued. "You accept our goods when they are not up to standard because you don't want us to lose out. But we want to increase our sales – we have thousands of skilled craftsmen who are out of work. How will we get into your high streets if we don't know what sort of quality your customers expect? Reject our goods if they are not up to standard! It will be better for us in the long run. We need to learn from you; we want our products to be of the best possible quality.

"That's not all," he went on, addressing those of us in particular from Europe and America. "What kind of image are we putting across when fair trade shops sell goods which aren't up to scratch, or when all the designs are out of date? It's not enough just to believe in what you're doing. We want you to be more professional, to market our products more effectively. *We need more orders!* Leaflets and campaigning are not enough! Fair trade food is booming – why are craft sales not booming too?"

As the millennium approached, change was on the agenda. People were talking about a new era; what would the future bring? The twenty-first century, the stuff of science fiction novels, was about to become

reality. It was a challenge, and fair trade organisations were responding in different ways.

Some, like Traidcraft, were concentrating on foods and the vast market that was opening up as the supermarkets became increasingly interested in fair trade. Food and coffee wholesalers like Cafédirect and Equal Exchange prospered. New ones like Divine Chocolate and Tropical Wholefoods grew fast. Traidcraft's new Geobar achieved sales of a million pounds in just one year.

Craft producers, however, were complaining that orders were static or decreasing. The UK's largest craft importer at the time, Oxfam, closed its 'fair trade only' shops (which did not sell donated goods) and made the hard decision to stop importing crafts, leaving several of its suppliers in the lurch. Producers could not understand this. They could see there was a vast potential for their products in the gift and fashion markets of the developed countries, but it wasn't being exploited.

Although new fair trade shops were opening, many tended to follow the same pattern. They were in poor locations, were staffed by volunteers and relied on a niche market of customers who already believed in fair trade. Food was one of the mainstays of their stock, and they were losing sales to the supermarkets. Visiting producers loved their atmosphere and commitment but found them lacking overall in comparison to high street gift-shops.

The first person to visit Shared Earth in the new millennium was Agung from Mitra Bali. He said he was "stunned" by the quality of goods we had on offer. He was "full of praise and enthusiasm" for Shared Earth – we had, after all, plied him with drink at a 'training session' in a local pub the previous evening. "It was a great experience," he wrote, "to get to know all of you, it was wonderful time, even though my body stabbed by the cold winter."

Despite such praise, and despite its paid staff and retail expertise, Shared Earth still had a long way to go. The challenge of the 1990s had been to survive, but now we had to expand our vision, appeal to as wide a range of customers as possible, and become even more professional. We had four shops in good locations, and were ideally suited to benefit some of the craft producers who were so desperate for orders.

I decided to increase our product range dramatically; the African

producer's appeal – *we need more orders* – was lodged firmly in my mind. Our wholesale catalogue was still largely restricted to recycled and handmade paper, wooden animals from Bali, and a few products from India. Why not diversify into other areas? In 2000, I appointed our first designer, Emma Jennings, to help with product development. The next IFAT conference was in Tanzania and I set off to it optimistically, hoping to find new suppliers for her to work with.

The journey began in Kenya, where I was staying with a cousin, Peter Davey and his wife Greta, who lived a few miles outside Nairobi. I was tired, and the bus from the city centre soon picked up speed.

"You must have a very efficient service here," I said to a fellow passenger. "It's great to be travelling so fast and not be stuck in traffic jams."

"Don't count your chickens!" he responded. "We have a lot of young bus drivers who take drugs, then they think they're James Bond and drive as fast as they can. Eighty percent of the accidents on this road are head-on collisions – there are fatalities every day!"

This was not reassuring. I looked at our driver. I couldn't tell if he was on drugs, but he certainly looked young. A few minutes later I was even more worried as we passed two crumpled cars by the side of the road, one of them blackened by fire. Medics were leaning over a body on the ground. Two policemen were doing their best to keep a crowd of onlookers away.

I reached my destination intact. I hadn't seen Peter for years and I had never met Greta. I soon discovered we had a mutual interest in environmental issues, and discussed the issue of 'shopping miles' and the importance of 'buying local.' Controversially, roses from Kenya, which are flown to the UK, have recently been given the Fairtrade mark, but these things aren't always as simple as they seem. Roses from Cornwall or Belgium are responsible for even higher CO_2 emissions than those flown from Kenya, because the greenhouses they are grown in have to be heated through the winter months. So perhaps the moral is: buy local in summer, and from Kenya in winter?

It's a big issue for the fair trade movement and there are no easy answers. The export of fruit, vegetables and flowers has been a real bonus for some very poor countries like Kenya, providing jobs to many people who would otherwise be struggling to survive. Many are perishable and have to be flown to the UK. It raises the question, what is more important: people or planet? If we buy local here, what happens to the millions of farm-workers who rely on exports for a living?

There's no definitive answer to this, but I do have strong feelings about what the fair trade movement should be doing as a whole. One of our key principles is that trade should be sustainable, and we ask a lot of our producers – are their raw materials renewable, are their dyes organic, is their waste disposed of correctly? – and so on. In Europe, America and other developed countries, however, we are often woefully inadequate. Many companies don't even have an Environmental Policy. We don't monitor our CO_2 emissions, we don't recycle enough waste, and we travel to meetings by air when we could go by train. We could be taking the lead on these issues, and we're not.

Greta showed me another side of the 'roses from Kenya' debate. The greenhouses in Kenya are heated by the sun, but the glass becomes murky and has to be replaced every few years. Usually it's thrown out, but Greta, who is in her seventies, has set up a project to collect it and give it to families in the Nairobi slums for use as building materials. When she learned about Shared Earth, she spotted another opportunity for recycling glass.

"I know just the thing for you," she said.

Next morning, after a breakfast of fresh fruit in her luxuriant garden, with exotic birds chattering in the bushes, we headed back to Nairobi, to the last place tourists would go – the city landfill site. A city official, dressed in a smart suit, accompanied us, looking rather worried in case his polished shoes got dirty. The heat was overpowering; the smell was even worse.

We were looking for a group of women from a nearby slum, who were collecting bottles to use as raw materials for making jewellery. They worked in the middle of the site, in a simple one-walled canvas structure held up with wooden posts to shade them from the sun. After collecting the used bottles, along with any pieces of china they could

find, they sorted them into colours, melted them down, and turned them into beads.

We found the women at last, and as the vultures flew overhead, saw several other groups of people, mostly women and children, collecting metal and other materials from the rubbish all around. Some were turned into crafts – like replica toys and bicycles made from recycled wire – which I later saw being sold in the streets to tourists.

Unfortunately, the group we were visiting had no experience of selling commercially, let alone exporting, and we didn't have the resources to help them. Nor did we know anyone else who could. It's one of the problems of fair trade. Most producers don't speak English; some are illiterate. Most work in small family groups or co-operatives, with little access to market trends, finance or business advice. To move beyond the local tourist market, they need someone with expertise to help them, like Asha Handicrafts or Mitra Bali.

Fair trade has a social purpose too, and that's one of the differences between fair trade and 'ethical' products. When a shop or business says its products have been ethically sourced, it usually means that minimum wages are being paid, health and safety laws are complied with, and children aren't exploited. It may also relate to environmental standards, depending on the products; in the case of wood, for instance, avoiding the use of hardwoods.

Fair trade goes that bit further. It's like a 'gold standard.' It aims not just to pay decent wages, but to benefit the most disadvantaged people – those at the bottom of the heap. Several fair trade organisations work with disabled people. One of Shared Earth's suppliers, Craft Aid in Mauritius, employs deaf and disabled workers. Another, New Sadle in Nepal, is a community for people with leprosy. Much of its income comes from the sale of bags, purses and other accessories. The residents are of all ages and contribute to production in whatever way they can. Even those who have no fingers or toes can operate looms by pushing handles or moving a foot pedal up and down. This gives them a purpose in life. People with severe illnesses or disabilities are often seen as a burden, but in workshops and communities like this they can regain their self-respect.

The primary aim of fair trade – as well as demonstrating an alternative

model of trade, of course – is to bring people out of poverty. It also aims to improve their confidence and help them to develop as people, so they can play a useful role in society. Fair trade organisations are usually involved in education, literacy, health and other social projects. When you buy a fair trade product, you contribute to these projects.

Unfortunately, neither Greta nor I could find an organisation in Nairobi which would be able to work with the women on the landfill site. They were from a nearby slum, and could hardly write their own names, let alone fill in complicated export documents. For us to buy from them, they needed someone local who could visit them regularly and help them to expand from selling in the street to exporting. All we could do was encourage them, tell them we liked their products – and move on. It happens often, and it's not easy. Unfortunately, helping the smallest groups, who need your help most, is sometimes just not possible.

From Nairobi I travelled by bus to the IFAT conference in Arusha, Tanzania. As we went further into the countryside the traffic, to my relief, thinned out. The trees, in contrast, became more abundant; near the city many are cut down for firewood. I saw the occasional giraffe and a few zebras. At the border I was surrounded by women in traditional Masai costume, waving crafts at me hopefully, but I could not buy everything. Soon I was in Arusha.

Conferences can be tedious. I suppose in most conferences there are people who get up and talk for ages, monopolising the debate. But in fair trade? It's not really fair, is it. I once got up and said so (briefly, I hope.) I could see one or two people looking a bit guilty. "Hmm. He's not implying that I like the sound of my own voice, is he? Maybe I have spoken once or twice too often. Hope people aren't connecting what he's saying with me. Don't want to be considered an *un*fair trader."

For the next ten minutes there was a pleasant silence after people spoke, as if everyone was considering what had been said, instead of jumping up to propound their own point of view. Then things went back to normal.

Outside the official debates, however, the Arusha conference was

excellent. By 2001, IFAT had grown substantially. It was a great opportunity to meet new producer groups and I made the most of it. Our current suppliers were in India, Sri Lanka, Indonesia and the Philippines. With the new contacts I made in Arusha, it wasn't long before we were importing from Bangladesh, Nepal, Vietnam, Zambia, Egypt, Kenya, Tanzania, Mexico and Peru as well. We soon had over twenty overseas suppliers, and I felt we were doing just a little bit more to answer that African producer's appeal, *we need more orders*. It was a bit of an experiment, and some of the new suppliers didn't work out, but at least we were trying.

It wasn't easy, because we were still short of capital. Importing is an expensive business. It's a principle of fair trade that when you place an order, you offer advance payment, usually half, so the producers can buy raw materials without having to borrow from money lenders. The remaining 50% is paid either when the goods are shipped, or when they arrive. This means you have to pay for everything before you've sold a single item. Production of handicrafts is time-consuming too, and they often take five months to arrive. If you're not careful, you may have a cash-flow crisis on your hands, especially if your wholesale customers don't pay their bills on time.

I was keen to buy from several of the producers I met at Arusha, but to order from all of them would be impossible. We just couldn't afford it. I came up with a plan: we would ask our customers to order in advance, so we knew exactly what to order. When the shipments arrived, we could then immediately send the goods out and invoice them. We would still have to pay in advance, but there would be no risk of our capital being tied up in our warehouse as dead stock. On the other hand, if the goods sold well, then we would have nothing left if customers wanted to re-order.

Our Advance Order Catalogue was released in January 2002 and exhibited at the Birmingham Spring Fair in February. It was full of exciting new crafts, including recycled tin from Kenya, woodcarvings from Tanzania and Lombok, hand-painted cushion covers from Zambia, glass from Mexico, and candles made from brazil nut husks from the Amazon forests of Peru. Twelve new suppliers were represented, including three from India. We also included new products from our

established suppliers, such as chess sets from Asha Handicrafts, which previously we thought would be too expensive. Now we could try them out without risk – we would only be ordering what our customers were committed to buy.

This expansion into so many new products, suppliers and countries was the most exciting thing that had happened at Shared Earth for many years. Change is important in business, and we were really moving forward and doing something positive to benefit producers across the world. We were importing lots of new, unusual products, some of which had never been seen in the UK before. From a financial point of view we would also benefit. Despite any cash flow problems, our profit should go up, because we would be buying direct instead of from other UK importers.

My enthusiasm was not shared by everyone, however. I was the 'bête noir' of our accounts office for many months, if not years. A special accounting system had to be set up, with detailed records for each customer. Deposits had to be collected, and customers who had forgotten to include them with their orders had to be chased. Then when the goods arrived, they all arrived at different times; you couldn't just invoice a customer once, you had to do it separately each time a new delivery came in. Sometimes the wrong quantities arrived, or a few products were damaged, and we had to decide which customers would receive what. Often the paperwork from the suppliers was incorrect.

"The administration of this scheme is an absolute nightmare," I was told. "It's alright for you. You just place the orders and leave it up to us. We have to deal with all the problems." For some time, I avoided going into our accounts office unless I really had to.

Despite this, the launch of the new catalogue was extremely successful; we took nearly £50,000 worth of orders at the Birmingham Spring Fair. It was equally valuable, however, as an experiment. The products in it were completely different from anything we had sold previously. They re-invigorated our shops, and we learned a great deal about what customers wanted.

The catalogue included our first products from New Delhi-based supplier Aspiration; many are still in our wholesale catalogue today, seven years later. Bags, bedspreads, cushion covers, furniture, woodcarvings,

Above My first IFAT conference in Maryland, USA, 1995.
Below Agung Alit, Michelle Hughes (designer) and Adi Komang Adrartha.

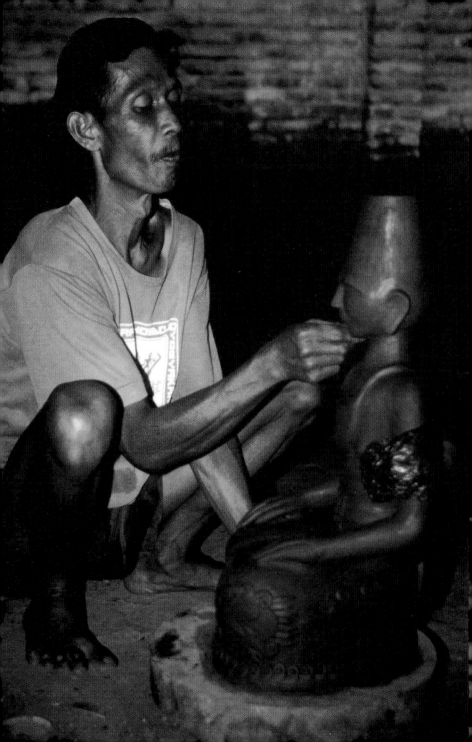

Left
Sri Lanka, 1995. I was invited into this family's house for a cup of tea.

Right
Gospel House - the wood arrives.

Opposite
Balinese woodcarver.

Left
Gospel House - an order of jigsaws is ready to be dispatched.

Right
Lucas Caldeira, Asha Handicrafts.

Opposite
Balinese woodcarver. It looks like a production line, but it's all done by hand.

Below
Gede Sukarsana (left) and his brother. He was able to build a new workshop as a result of our orders.

Left
SHAPII workers making paper

Below left
Loreta Rafisura

Below centre
Fair Trade goes contemporary: Animal Magic 'traditional' papier maché boxes.
Sarah Morris was our shop manager for many years.

Above right
Balinese craftswoman painting cats.

Right
Itxaso (designer) with Padam (right) and Kantha.

Above
Saharanpur: shesham wood
arrives for auction.

Right
Peruvian master-potter.

Below
Gulfam carving wooden frames.

Above
People suffering from leprosy
find work and a home at
New Sadle, Nepal.

Right
Itxaso helps GET Paper,
Nepal to design new stationery.

Left
Vietnamese
craftswomen in
traditional dress.

Left

Fulmaya Lama (in black jacket) with two other seamstresses from the Suryamuki Girls' Group, near Kathmandu.

Below

Chakkali Bal was abducted, at the age of fifteen, into a brothel. She was eventually rescued and now campaigns tirelessly on behalf of those who have contracted AIDS in similar circumstances.

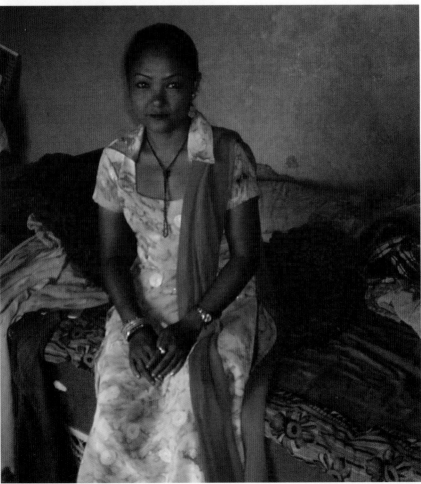

Above Children at Karm Marg with Jo Wakefield, one of Shared Earth's designers.

Left and below Children at Karm Marg.

Left Dev Sethi, one of the founders of Karm Marg.

Is it possible that they could turn into adults like these?
Four ex-street children who now run Karm Marg's workshops.
Above Left Rakesh **Above Right** Rumpi **Below Left** Arti **Below Right** Payal.

Opposite
The Mumbai Marathon, January 2007.
Sarah and I are on the left.

Left
The money Asha raised from the marathon enabled
children like Suman to go to school when
their parents would otherwise have not
been able to afford it.

Below
'National Dress' at IFAT conference,
Belgium 2007. Left to right, Indonesia,
Nepal, Ghana and Britain - jeans and trainers!

Left
Ardesh and Moon
from Tara with Itxaso
and myself. Moon is a
tireless campaigner
against child labour
in India. I am wearing
my skinny-necked
jumper from Dilli
Haat!

Above One of Tara's schools in the Indira Camp slum, New Delhi.
The youngsters sit at the front, the older children and adults at the back.
Below Many of the women at Indira Camp work as packers at Tara Projects;
some are now learning to make jewellery too.

Above Solar cookers at EMA, Kolkata.
Rice and vegetables take about an hour to cook.
Below Lynne Dawson, Shared Earth's
Retail Manager, travelled to India in 2007.

Above Learning to be a silversmith, Jaipur 2006. Since then,
the price of silver has rocketed and many craftsmen have had to change their jobs.

Below Fair trade moves on! Master craftsmen
Bashir Ahmed pictured on a bus to promote fair trade in Nottingham.

nativity sets, wallhangings, candles, ceramics – we had never imported any of these before. The Advance Order scheme was soon discontinued, but it was the basis for a huge expansion in our craft ordering. Our wholesale catalogue trebled from 48 to 156 pages over the next four years. As it grew, we expanded our design team, taking on two more designers to liaise with suppliers and develop more of our own unique products.

★☆★

One of our new suppliers was in a country I had never visited before, Vietnam. I had talked with Tran Lan, the manager of Craftlink, at the IFAT conference in Arusha. Craftlink, like Asha and Mitra Bali, acts as a go-between to facilitate trade between small producers and buyers abroad, advising the producers and handling the paperwork and invoicing. Their stall at the conference 'marketplace', a kind of mini-trade show for IFAT members, stood out immediately. They had such high quality products that I resolved to visit them to meet their producers and see what else was available.

It's always exciting when you set off on a journey to a country you've never been to before. I was especially excited to be visiting Vietnam in 2001 as it's a small country which fought the power of America. During my youth, it was an icon of hope, suffering, atrocity and resistance. As I got off the plane at Hanoi, I didn't know what to expect. It was a communist country and I was apprehensive about the welcome I would receive. I needn't have worried. My anxiety was dispelled on the first night, as I left my hotel to look for somewhere to eat.

"Hallo!" called a man in a grey boiler-suit, who was sitting at a table on the pavement. Three other men, also dressed in boiler-suits, sat with him. "What is your name?"

This was the limit of their English, but I gathered that they were electricians. They insisted that I join them. This was not easy, because the chairs, made of red plastic, were more like stools from a kindergarten, and the table was about the height of a normal chair seat.

I was also unsure of my position, because this was Hanoi, and the legacy of the Vietnam War was still evident: people were still being

maimed by unexploded bombs in the fields. The electricians didn't know if I was an American or not. But it didn't matter. They smiled as if I was a long-lost brother, without a trace of suspicion or enmity in their faces. They were ready to welcome me, whatever my nationality.

The table was empty, and I wasn't sure if they'd just finished their meal or were about to start. Soon, however, a calor gas burner, with a powerful flame underneath, arrived on the table, similar to those you're given in Asian restaurants to keep the food warm. A large aluminium pot full of water was placed on it, and we waited for it to boil. Then a huge bundle of some kind of green vegetable, a bit like spinach, was brought to the table.

One of the electricians placed a handful of the greens in the boiling water – to which, I discovered, some kind of flavouring had already been added – and in a couple of minutes we were all dipping into it with our chopsticks. Every few minutes the owner of the 'restaurant' (which was in a nearby alley and consisted of a table, a washing up bowl and a few boxes) brought along a bowl of something else – seafood, noodles, vegetables, all uncooked – which we added to the pot to replenish its contents.

The dish became a delightful mixture of different foods, changing its flavour as each new ingredient was added. Although we could not speak each other's language, it was an excellent social occasion, and the electricians and I parted good friends. I could not have had a warmer welcome to the country.

Next day I attended Craftlink's annual bazaar where over forty producer groups were displaying their wares. It was a wonderful opportunity to see what was available and to meet the producers, some of whom had come from the remotest areas of the country. The day after that I was on the road with Lan, visiting some of the ones I had favoured most. The country was green and lush, and everyone was friendly. Nearly thirty years earlier, in 1974, I had sat in King's Square in York as a student, waving banners to protest against the Vietnam war. Hard to imagine that now I was sitting in someone's living room near Hanoi, drinking tea and discussing how he lacquered his bamboo pots.

Soon I was placing orders for hemp bags, cushion covers, smoked bamboo furniture, traditional water puppets, ornate woodcarvings and a

variety of other products. Craftlink received more orders than any other supplier in our Advance Order Catalogue. They were too unusual to be mass sellers, and the high prices – which reflected the fair wages and the high level of craftsmanship – were pushing them towards the luxury end of the market.

In fair trade we always aim to create long-term relationships with our suppliers, but it's hard to do this with crafts. You can sell tea and coffee and chocolate for ever; you might want to change the packaging from time to time, but the basic product is still the same. Crafts have to be constantly redesigned, and fashions change every year. When I started Shared Earth, jute baskets and sikas from Bangladesh were all the rage. In the early 90s, African crafts took off; everyone was buying Kisii stone sculptures and wooden masks. Then no-one wanted them any more. For the next few years everyone was buying crafts from Bali. In the late 90s, Vietnam became popular for a while, then handmade cards, which previously people wouldn't touch with a bargepole. Today, jute is back in fashion as people switch from plastic to long-life bags. How do you decide how long a trend will last? It's one of the hardest jobs a business has to face.

It's even more difficult when you're buying new products from a new country. You just have to try things out and see what happens. Unfortunately, the products we bought from Craftlink didn't take off as we had hoped. Orders to another supplier, Mai Vietnamese Crafts in Ho Chi Minh City, were more successful, and we place orders to this day.

Ordering directly meant better profits, because we were cutting out the UK middlemen. There were risks, however. One shipment in particular was a disaster. We ordered a container of woodcarvings from Ghana. For months, we eagerly awaited their arrival; like the products from Craftlink, they were completely different from anything else we had. When the boxes were opened, we found everything was so covered in mould that you couldn't tell one product from the next. The wood had not been treated properly, and the whole consignment had to be incinerated.

2002 was not a good year for Shared Earth. Although sales went up, our costs went up even more. We had too many office staff, and narrowly avoided making a loss. The more we imported directly from overseas, however, the more our profit margins increased. Although things were tight, we were more secure than we had been in the 1990s. I began to start thinking about opening another shop. This, I reasoned, would spread our office costs between five shops instead of four, making the whole business more viable.

The opportunity came the following year, purely by chance. I had never visited one of our best wholesale customers, Fair Do's in Cardiff, and decided it was time I did so. When I arrived I discovered it was in a suburb, a long way from the city centre, where there wasn't a fair trade shop at all. I had some time to spare before my train left; why not have a look around? I soon came across an empty shop in the Royal Arcade. Planning is all very well in business, but sometimes things just happen. In less than a month I had signed the lease.

As Shared Earth expanded, one of my roles had been travelling round our shops to see that all was well. It was a time-consuming job, and with five shops it would be even more difficult. I also wanted to concentrate more on buying. Lynne was promoted to Retail Manager, overseeing all the shops. Our staff became used to her sharp eyes. She was especially keen to point out gaps in our display, where products had been sold and not replaced.

"You can't sell things from the stockroom," she repeated again and again, especially to new staff. It was a kind of mantra, like 'retail is detail' or 'location, location, location.' She says she got it from me.

"I got really fed up with you when I started at Shared Earth," she told me. "You kept coming in and saying, 'you can't sell things from the stockroom, you can't sell things from the stockroom.' I could have wrung your neck.

"Eventually," she continued, on a conciliatory note, "I realised it was often the bestsellers that had sold. That's obvious really – because they're bestsellers, they're much more likely to sell. I don't need to tell you that." (Lynne is very good at adding remarks like this to her conversation. She knows I'm easily flattered). "So we had all these bestsellers sitting in the stockroom, which weren't out on the shelves, and it was having a real

effect on our sales." I smiled. "You were right, as it happens," she added, as if that was a rare event.

Cardiff was a challenge, and she quickly got stuck in.

"We need shelves in the storeroom, a new counter, repairs to the floor and goodness knows what else," she told her husband David, a retired chef. "I know you'll help out, won't you…"

It was an order, not a question. It wasn't long till Christmas, and he was hardly allowed to leave the premises. Within two weeks, we were open. It was a historic occasion, the first time in ten years that we had opened a new shop.

Hundreds of millions of skilled people in developing countries are unemployed, underemployed or employed in exploitative conditions. It was a drop in the ocean, but our new Cardiff shop would be another small response to that plea, *we need more orders*.

13 The Railway Children

ON A RECENT visit to Kolkata I walked past a room which opened on to the street where children aged ten to thirteen were making clothes. To create more space, the room had been divided in half, horizontally, making two 'floors', each about four feet high. The children had to stoop whenever they left their sewing machines. About ten children were crowded on to each 'floor.'

They were like battery hens, except the product was clothes, not eggs, and I was looking at children, not hens. Strange that we care so much about free range eggs, and yet have so little idea about the extent of child labour in India, where many of our clothes are made. It's not just the odd sweatshop here and there. Up to 100 million children are said to be involved; a staggering number. Sometimes they are made to work as much as sixteen or eighteen hours in a day.

To raise awareness of these kind of issues, Lynne often gives talks to schools and community groups. Recently, she tried to convert the residents of a women's refuge in Stockport, near Manchester, to fair trade. Her talk did not go well.

"It was like tea-break time at the local Puppy Stranglers' Association," she told me. "I wasn't getting through at all."

It was Fair Trade Fortnight, and she was hoping the women might sympathise with the plight of impoverished women and children in countries like India.

"It couldn't be more difficult than it is 'ere," said a woman with a

shaved head and scars on her face. "What d'yer think we have to put up with?"

"Well, they have stopped burning widows on pyres, it's true," retorted Lynne.

You can't deny the suffering of women and children who end up in a refuge, of course, and fair trade is about alleviating suffering, but fair trade doesn't attempt to tackle the problems of people in rich countries. It's been suggested that the Fairtrade Mark should be available to Welsh hill farmers who are struggling to make a living. Although things may be difficult for them, they still have a good state social security system to rely on. In many countries, if there's a drought or if crops fail, farmers and their children starve.

When you've seen the suffering of such people, and want to do something to help, it's hard to know what's right if you live in the developed world. Should you give your possessions away and live on the basics, just enough to survive, to show you don't want to benefit from your country's inherited wealth and power? It would be a gesture of solidarity. But would anyone notice? Would it help to change the world?

I went along this route for many years. I gave away most of my few possessions. Moving house became easy; clothes, pots and pans – they all fitted into the boot of a friend's car. Then gradually over the years I started accumulating things again. A house, furniture, household accessories, a TV, and then a bigger one: where does it all stop? Sometimes I wonder if I've gone down the wrong track.

Fair trade is not about giving everything up, though. It's not even about equality – we don't say in fair trade that everyone should have the same. We say that trade should be fair, and that we all deserve to have the basic necessities of life – enough to eat, clothes on our backs and a reasonable place to live. We should be able to send our children to school, receive decent medical care and earn enough to save for retirement. Beyond that, what we do with our lives is up to us. If we become rich, it should not be at the expense of others becoming poor.

Much of our wealth in Europe and North America has been acquired by exploiting the labour of people in our former colonies. Should we give it back? Complex theories can be woven about the way the world

developed as it did, the reasons why some nations are poor and others rich. I'm not the kind of person who can argue all the details. I just know that when people work long hours in dreadful conditions, for a pittance, and the companies that sell their goods make billions – then it's wrong. When most of us in Britain can afford to buy more clothing than we will ever wear, when the prices are low because it's made in sweatshops by children – that's wrong. We have a debt to pay the Third World. We have a responsibility to see that things change.

Poverty is not necessary. It's no more necessary than the exploitation of children was in Britain in the nineteenth century. It could be eradicated easily – throughout the world – if international trade were conducted more fairly. It would not require great personal sacrifices. The average household in Britain throws away over £400 worth of food in a year. What a waste! That's more than most families earn in a year in many developing countries. If we cut down that waste, and spent the money saved on more fair trade products, it would be just one thing we could do to improve the lot of those who make the food we eat.

None of us want people abroad to starve. We've shown, by our support for fair trade food, that we're prepared to pay a bit more. But that's just on a personal level. To eradicate poverty we need government action.

Sainsbury's have shown that it's possible to sell fair trade food at normal prices. Their fair trade bananas are often cheaper than in local markets. It's a great example of what one supermarket can do, and still their sales and profits go up. Multinational companies make enormous profits; a fairer share should go back to the producers.

As individuals, we are voting with our wallets by buying fair trade products. Politicians know this. They should heed our call. We need legislation now, to make the terms of trade fairer between the rich and poor countries of the world.

We dallied with going back to fair trade food, as we had done when One World first opened, but the supermarkets – in conjunction with the Fairtrade Mark – were doing too good a job at stocking Fairtrade food. Instead, we moved into new recycled products made in the UK.

Wine glasses made from bottles sliced in half; stationery made from old computer circuit boards; mouse mats made from rubber tyres – all sold well as awareness of global warming grew.

We were still buying from a number of UK importers. Some had impeccable credentials, but three or four weren't doing anything special. They weren't exploiting people, but they weren't committed to fair trade, to going out of their way to buy from the people who needed orders most. Gradually, we weeded them out and replaced them with our own suppliers, most of them members of IFAT.

Our main UK supplier, Windhorse Trading, bought mainly from Indonesia, Thailand and the Far East. They were a commercial wholesaler, but they were also a Buddhist organisation, concerned about ethical issues. Were they concerned about the same issues we are in the fair trade movement?

Buddhists often say that life is suffering, caused by human traits like greed, hatred and disillusion. The way out, for a Buddhist, is to free yourself from attachment; it's a personal journey, a personal mission. As part of this journey, Buddhists do all they can to alleviate the suffering of others.

Could Windhorse guarantee their producers were not being exploited? Were children working in sweatshops, or craftsmen toiling for long hours for low wages to make their products?

"Buddhism is not an abstract philosophy," said Bob Jones, their Managing Director. "You're continually working out how to apply Buddhist teaching to every aspect of your daily life. 'Don't hurt people – help them': we've always tried to work like that. Contact with Shared Earth has made us think about the details more. You asked us questions which we couldn't answer – whether women were being paid the same as men, for instance. It helped us to audit our suppliers better."

We admired Windhorse for their honesty and openness. Being transparent about what you're doing is one of the principles of fair trade. They published a guide to their suppliers, dropped one of their main Indian suppliers, whose ethical performance they were unhappy about, and placed a large order with one of our fair trade suppliers in New Delhi.

✶ᛁ✶

In 2005, it was time for another IFAT conference, and this time it was in Quito, the capital of Ecuador. My mind turned to food again. We had a day off for cultural activities, and about thirty of us took a coach into the countryside. We had been invited to a peasant co-operative for lunch. They were poor people and had gone to great trouble to provide us with their national speciality: roast guinea pig.

On the way to the co-operative, to acquaint us with the industry, we had been taken to a guinea pig processing factory. Apparently, large quantities are exported to Ecuadorian communities in the USA. The factory was a model of job creation, excellent conditions and worker participation. I looked round the door, and decided not to go in. Half an hour later, as my companions came out, they told me I had made the right decision. I saw green faces, and someone heading for a nearby bush.

We arrived at the peasant hacienda. The roast guinea pig was piled up high in a huge serving basket, along with others containing sweetcorn and potatoes. I thought of the two guinea pigs I had kept as pets as a child.

There was clearly going to be some kind of ceremony before the meal, I assumed some kind of grace, but this went back further in time than the Spanish conquistadores, perhaps even to before Christianity itself. Putting our hands on the shoulder of the person in front, we snaked slowly round the tables of food, bending backwards and forwards at the waist and with each step bellowing rhythmically, "HOO, ha, ha, HOO, ha, ha, HOO, ha, ha." The cauldron of roast guinea pig emitted an intoxicating smell as we passed it. If a witch-doctor in a hairy mask had leapt out and danced round with us, waving a skull in the air, it would not have seemed out of place.

Then it was time to eat. Would it be noticed if I left out the roast guinea pig, which our hosts were offering us so proudly? Fortunately, I was not the only guest who was reluctant to put any on their plate. If I was offending our hosts, at least half the other guests were as well, and not just the vegetarians from India. The baskets of potatoes and sweetcorn – a variety about four times as big as the one we see in Britain – were

emptying fast. I breathed a sigh of relief that I wasn't the only one going for the veggie option.

✳✦✳

Not long after I was back in India, with its strange mixture of new wealth and millions of people just eking out a living. Many will do anything they can – exploiting children if necessary – to escape from poverty. As a well-off European, you would expect to be in danger of being mugged at any moment. Yet I feel safer in Indian cities than I do in London. On my first visit to Asha Handicrafts, I stayed in a rickety hotel next to a large slum. The area was characterised by dim street lights, open sewers and refuse in the streets.

I went for a walk in the evening; it was about ten o'clock. As I walked further into the slum, the street lights became even dimmer, and in places non-existent. Suddenly I was approached by a gang of teenagers, who stopped and surrounded me.

"What is your name? Where you from?" they asked. I tried to respond in a friendly way, and asked them their names in return. "Arpka nam kya hai?" It was about the limit of my Hindi at the time. They laughed. My pronunciation was a cause for great hilarity.

Then they spotted my camera. One of them held his hand out. It was not an expensive camera, to me at any rate. To these boys, it could be worth three months' wages – the equivalent of thousands of pounds. It was clear from their clothing that they were not well off.

My first thought was to assume that was the end of my camera, and to wonder if I would be mugged for my wallet as well. The street was practically deserted, the road cracked and refuse-strewn, the nearest street-lamp fifty yards away. Yet something inside me told me I needn't worry. I handed the camera over. It was passed round and admired – then handed back.

In England, where we have so much, we lock all our doors and barely talk to people in the street any more. I would not feel safe handing my camera over to street-kids in London, especially to a gang of youths at night. Our consumerist lifestyles lead to greed, stress, and unhappiness. One person told me that in India, older men keep their hair, but when they come to England, they go bald…

"Fair trade is not just about money," Stephen Thomas of Tearcraft told me at a recent IFAT conference. "It's about dignity, about valuing people for what they are and not what they possess. If you have the basics in life, you can be happy. In Britain and America, consumerism has gone wild, and we forget the importance of relationships and community."

Moon Sharma from Tara Projects in New Delhi agreed.

"If you hurt someone by taking their money, it has no value," she said. "When I first came to Europe I thought it was heaven. Later, I had a different perspective. In the West you have a different kind of poverty. I had a friend in Denmark who took me to see her mother, who was in a sheltered home. She visited her once each month. It was very nice, but it was a shock, because everyone there just seemed to be waiting to die. Her mother wanted to be with her family. This was real poverty. My friend was giving money to Mother Theresa, but she hardly saw her own mother at all. You need people to talk to and love; it's human relations that make you rich."

Moon is passionate about opposing child labour, and staff at Tara have risked their lives taking hidden cameras into workshops where children are employed, to expose them and publicise the issue of child exploitation.

The Indira Camp tuition school is one of many schools set up by Tara. It doesn't have walls or a roof. It consists of a concrete slab, a blackboard and a few books. Indira Camp is a slum where three hundred families live, one family to a room. There's no running water, and the communal taps only come on for an hour in the morning and evening. The electrical supply is haphazard.

Yet there's a great community spirit in the slum; you sense it when you visit the school, which Tara started in 1998. The children are mostly of primary school age, but there are a few teenagers too, and in the same class you may also see women of thirty, fifty and seventy, all learning the same lesson. They all sit on rush mats on the floor, reciting their A-B-Cs, in both Hindi and English. Their faces glow proudly when a visitor appears.

"It's wonderful to be able to write my own name," said Sarvari Begum, who came to New Delhi from a village in the countryside, and was illiterate when she married at the age of eighteen. She was one of

the first pupils at the school. Now her ten-year old son is doing well at the local state school and she has high hopes for his future.

Jagwali Devi, another inhabitant and ex-pupil, agrees, saying it opened "a new face of life" when she was able to read the numbers of buses and where they were going. Now 37, she has four children, a son and three daughters. She had no opportunity to go to school herself, but made sure her own children didn't miss out, despite the opposition of her husband, an alcoholic, who was unable to provide enough money even for simple meals. She earned about forty rupees a day (50p) cleaning vegetables for a wholesaler when the work was available.

Eventually, through the Indira Camp school, she came into contact with Tara Projects, where she doubled her income immediately. She has now worked for Tara for twelve years as a packer.

"I was happy when I came into contact with Tara. Their social workers made us aware about the importance of education. They arranged literacy classes for the children and women in the community. It was a great joy for us. Since I didn't know how to read and write I joined the classes in spite of resistance from my husband. Today I can take better care of my basic accounts; I get work support from Tara and have learnt how to assemble bead bracelets. I earn minimum 100 rupees per day and I can save money through our self-help group, initiated with the help of Tara's social workers. My daughters are also attending secondary school regularly."

Sarvari and Jagwali both comment on how the school and the support of Tara has helped to build up their confidence.

"I will be attached to Tara until the day I die," Sarvari told me. "I don't want to go to any other place. Moon listens to my problems if I have any and I'm able to earn enough to support my family. She has helped me to build up my confidence and to stand on my own feet. Earlier I would have been very shy. I've opened up – previously I was confined to home and wouldn't mix with people easily. I wouldn't have been able to visit a hospital on my own, for instance. Moon has also helped me to open a bank account and now I have savings."

As Stephen from Tearcraft told me – fair trade is not just about money. It enables people to become strong, to grow as people, to respect themselves and learn to deal with problems. It helps them to feel part

of a community. In turn, it may help them to be more compassionate to
others.

Like Asha Handicrafts, Tara Projects exports crafts on behalf of a
number of producer groups. Its specialities are soapstone and jewellery.
Shared Earth placed its first order with Tara in 2003, and its jewellery was
an instant success. Today it takes up almost a quarter of our wholesale
catalogue, and provides a multi-coloured array of necklaces, bracelets
and earrings in our shops.

The Indira Camp school and others like it set up by Tara were inspired
by the Gandhian ideal of lifting people above the poverty line and
training them in skills so they can earn a living for themselves and be
self-sufficient. In every town in Britain, especially on a Saturday, you
see crowds of teenagers going into chain-stores like Accessorize and
Monsoon to buy fashion jewellery. Now crowds of them come into
Shared Earth and spend their pocket money on Tara's jewellery instead.
It's a great feeling to know that all that money is benefiting people like
Sarvari, Jagwali and the children of the Indira Camp slum. Tara Projects
is one of the best examples in the world of a fair trade business which is
totally dedicated to social justice.

✖✗✖

Karm Marg, another of Shared Earth's suppliers, only moved into
trade by chance; it started with children. In fact, the children started
Karm Marg, which means 'the path of action.' They were living on New
Delhi Railway Station. With the help of Veena Lal, a social worker, they
started a small kitchen on a nearby street to prepare food for the children
living there. It was funded with money earned by the older children –
sometimes through stealing or pick-pocketing.

Around 300,000 children roam and work the streets of New Delhi.
They come from all over the country, mostly from rural India. Some
have run away from difficult or abusive circumstances at home; others
are lured by the glitz and glamour of the big city.

When they arrive, the fight for survival begins. At railway stations
and bus terminals, typical entry points for most of them, girls are often
picked up and forced into becoming sex workers. Boys start by finding

petty work in exchange for food. They work at the bottom of the station's jungle hierarchy, which consists of corrupt police, porters, tea and snack vendors, small time drug peddlers and the assorted group of people you always find in such places, exploiting and abusing these children for their advantage or personal pleasure. It is common knowledge that all young children living in and around the station are regularly sodomised, in return for buying some kind of security, food or possibly just one more day's survival. The struggle is harshest for the younger children, some of whom are as young as three or four.

The kitchen started in 1997 and soon Veena found the back-room of a house to use as a day-care centre. A few months later Devendra Sethi, a photographer and theatre specialist, became involved.

"I met Veena at a workshop I was running for the children at a colony of snake-charmers, and she took me to see the children at the railway station afterwards. There were thirty or forty of them, screaming, dancing around – there was a lot of energy there and it felt good. So I came back. I had been living in a spiritual community at Auroville and had only just arrived in Delhi. I felt what I had been learning was confined to philosophy – I needed to apply it in real life. Delhi is an aggressive city and it was a shock seeing how people treat each other.

"Once I got involved with the children, it just kept increasing. We had a weekly meeting with them, dealing with problems on the platform, that sort of thing. I was staying temporarily at an ashram for teachers and one of the children asked me, 'if you don't have a place to stay, why don't you come and live with us?' So I did.

"Some of the children had started sleeping in the backyard of the house if they were sick, and by this time there were about thirty-five of them there. In October, we had a fight with the older boys. Some girls had joined them and they were complaining because some of the boys were abusing them. We had to ask them to leave. Street children aren't accepted as children – they're considered more like aliens, as if they shouldn't be seen on the face of the earth. Abuse is common. It's worse for the girls.

"We had no money so we discussed with the children what we could do to give them a better future. A lot of them wanted to stay together and live on the streets together; there was hope there that they could improve

their lives. So Veena and I started talking to people and eventually we managed to find a room we could have permanently in Faridabad, about forty kilometres from New Delhi. It would give them security, especially the younger ones. Some of them were interested in studying. Initially it was for twenty-four children only. We borrowed five thousand rupees (£60), hired a van, and moved out there.

"In the morning when I woke up all the kids had gone! I didn't know where they were. I found them running about in the open fields like wild horses. They were free! There were no more adults bossing them around or threatening them any more. They were laughing and shouting with joy.

"All the kids have come from some kind of difficult family background. Living together was like a small community; they all participated and took responsibility. They had learned how to survive on the streets, but now it was time to move forward. That winter they all slept hugging each other because they didn't have any warm clothes, and kept getting up and moving around to keep warm.

"We started getting donations but we didn't want donations to pay for our everyday expenses. In 1998 we bought some sewing machines and the older boys learnt how to make jute bags. They were also making bags from recycled newspapers and selling them to shops, and soon we began making greetings cards and even some pottery. We had a stall at Dilli Haat and raised 45,000 rupees (£560) – it was unbelievable.

"We talked with the kids about getting more space and a proper home. Some of them were a bit scared by the idea, so we asked them what they wanted. They came up with all sorts of crazy and amazing ideas. Some interesting ones, too. They wanted very high walls so people couldn't disturb them, and security guards at the door. It was their insecurity. But they had aspirations just the same as other kids, like a TV room, a swimming pool and things like that – not all of them possible!

"Sales of the bags were going up and by 2000 we were able to buy an acre and a half of farmland. It was another two years before we had enough money to start building on it. The kids were involved in every aspect of it, starting with the design – we encouraged them to tell us what they wanted, there was no such thing as a bad question or a bad idea. And if they didn't like anything, they said so. When we had it

all worked out the older ones helped with the construction, while the younger ones did things like planting trees. Eventually we moved in, with 48 kids, in 2002.

"The kids are involved with everything, they even discuss things like the wages of the staff. It's about taking responsibility. You learn how to clean your bathroom, wash your clothes and how to cook. Even the youngest children have to look after their personal hygiene. Then as they get older, they receive vocational training – life skills, really – in things like carpentry, metal-work, stitching, silk-screen printing and so on – and they can help contribute to Karm Marg's income as well as going to school.

"It's not all about money – it's about learning to look after yourself. But we reward them financially, too. When they start producing goods which we can sell to our customers, we save money in their name so when they eventually leave, they'll have some savings to buy a place to live, set themselves up in work or whatever.

"Boys and girls living together is unusual, it's still not acceptable in wider society. But all families consist of males and females living together, so it's only natural that we should do the same; we're a home, not an orphanage. We have had problems; occasionally a girl gets pregnant and has a child. If this happens we encourage them to marry and try to help them financially to set up as a family. Then they have to stand on their own feet, but they know they will still be a part of our family here and will always have our support."

The home is called Karm Goan, which means 'the work village.' It's a space for the children to live, study, work and play together, and as befits its residents, who have struggled to find food and a place to sleep on the railway station, the crafts it sells are the product of high ingenuity and insufficient resources. Most are from recycled materials, whether it's old newspapers or textile scraps. Women from local villages help to collect the materials but the workshops themselves are managed by the older children. Payal, eighteen, is in charge of stationery; Arti, eighteen, manages the carpentry workshop. Rakesh, twenty-two, joined Karm Marg aged twelve. Now he's a full-time member of staff and looks after paper bag production. Their lives have turned around completely, from no-hope to hope.

"I want to be a professional designer," says Rumpi, nineteen, who manages the sewing workshop. "Then I'm going to start my own boutique." She says it in such a confident way that you really believe she will succeed. Other children want to be teachers, social workers, and managers.

"Our dream is to spread the spirit of innovation at a grassroots level," says Dev. "Then only will we address the problems of huge migration to our overcrowded mega-cities, and create a culture of self-employment linked to the mainstream sector in innovative ways."

Shared Earth was Karm Marg's first major overseas customer, and helped them to move a little bit closer to the mainstream by wholesaling their products in the UK. Unfortunately, our orders were limited. I still wanted to expand, to increase orders to all our suppliers.

On 10 November, 1986 our first shop had opened in Goodramgate, York. Twenty years later, on 10 November, 2006, I was sitting in our office, telling our bank manager (somewhat belatedly) that we had opened two more shops. One, in a large shopping mall in Bristol, had only opened the previous week. There's always a mixture of excitement and anxiety when you open a new shop. How will customers respond? What will the sales be like? In Bristol, they were neither good nor bad. It was a reasonable start; I was content.

The other shop was in Bold Street in Liverpool, and opened at the beginning of September. We took it over from another fair trade shop, Bold Justice. They had been open for almost as long as Shared Earth, but had fallen on hard times. A rent review was imminent, and its management committee were afraid it would not be able to keep going when the new rent came into place. They were thinking of closing.

It was run by a paid manager, three paid part-time staff, and a number of volunteers. To cover wages for all the staff as well as the impending rent increase, Shared Earth would need to increase Bold Justice's annual turnover of £130,000 to at least £200,000. It was a challenge, but we thought we could do it. After lengthy talks the transfer went ahead.

We kept the paid staff, appointed an Assistant Manager, and refitted

the shop, making the display look more attractive. But the main change was in the stock. Bold Justice had clung on to several suppliers for years, including fair trade food that was easily available in the supermarkets, and large African woodcarvings which no-one wanted to buy. Other shelves were half empty. We filled them up with new products from new suppliers.

Sales in the first two months were excellent. At the end of the first year we found we had not just reached our sales target, but more than doubled Bold Justice's sales to £300,000.

How did the staff from Bold Justice respond? The volunteers had all gone; four paid staff were left, including the manager, Sheila Reid. After some initial trepidation, they were encouraged, even excited by the way sales had taken off. Response from previous customers was positive and lots of new customers were coming in. It took time to get used to Shared Earth's way of doing things, but Sheila, who was close to retirement, immersed herself in the task of making the new shop a success, and moulded the old and new staff into a great new team.

Although obviously we were delighted by all of this, it was, I thought, a sad commentary on missed opportunities for fair trade shops in Britain generally. Whilst some have improved immensely, others, like so many poor people in the countries we buy from, are struggling to survive, and don't seem to know what to do. Whether it's insufficient resources or skills, unwillingness to invest, or just a fear of change, many shops are not reaching their full potential.

The challenge of producers, *we need more orders,* is not being met. Fair trade is not all about money – but in Britain and other developed countries, it's definitely about selling. It's about persuading people to spend as much of their money as possible on fair trade products. It doesn't matter if it's farmers in the countryside or children on New Delhi railway station – the more fair trade products are bought, the more we can alleviate the suffering of the people who need it most.

14 The Mumbai Marathon

YOU'VE GOT TO be pretty desperate to sell your child, but in Nepal I discovered this happens all too often. Fulmaya Lama was a Nepalese girl who suffered such a fate, and escaped. She tells the story in her own words:

"My name is Fulmaya Lama and now I am 19 years of age. I was born in a poor family of Hadikhola VDC. We didn't have much land for cultivation so we always had hand to mouth problem. When I was very small, I was very much interested to go school with other many of my friends who used to go school, but I had never seen school because of my poverty. Instead of going school I had to go for labour work so that my family could earn some money. As usual I was passing my days, one day one of our nearby relative made me agree to go to work in an Indian circus called Jamuna Circus.

"I went along with him when I was 11 years of age. I had lots of dream when I came to work in a circus. I was thinking to earn lots of money for my parents but within a week I knew that my dream would never fulfil because I knew that I was sold for some money in this circus. After a week my difficulties had started, actually I don't like to remember those days. I was beaten by iron stick so many times and I had to work in circus as a slave.

"Even though I was bought to work in circus I had to do body massage of owner's wife. If I denied doing that, I was beaten and had to sleep without food. We only got 10 to 15 rupees per month. The days were

passing and I became so frosted and became hopeless about meeting my family.

"Luckily once our circus came in to Nepal and I escaped from circus, at that time I had no money to pay bus fare but I explained my story and became able to return back home. While I returned back I came in contact of Suryamukhi Girls' Group and they explained about Group. I was very impressed and they enrolled me as a member of this girls' group. Slowly I started to adjust myself in the village and now I am actively involving in Group's income generating activities through tailoring activities."

The Suryamukhi Girls' Group was started by GET Paper, a handmade paper workshop in a romantic setting in the hills near Kathmandu. It's a co-operative with 125 members, mostly low income women from the surrounding villages. Nepal is one of the poorest countries in the world, and the regular income that GET Paper's members receive allows them to feel secure about basic needs like food and housing. GET Paper also supports the local community by planting trees and building schools, focusing in particular on girls with its 'Send Your Daughter To School' campaigns. It's active in the broader community too, raising awareness about AIDS through its charitable arm, GWP, which receives 40% of its profits.

Surrounded by rice fields, and with only a dirt track road leading up to it, you feel as a visitor that you are in a different world. The paper-making workshops contain no heavy machinery, indeed hardly any machinery at all. The materials which go into the mixing troughs are local agricultural waste like banana fibre, straw and water hyacinth, and the paper sheets are lifted from the trough by hand and dried in the sun. The noise of traffic is gone, and only the occasional sound of a dog barking disturbs the quiet. Labourers in the fields work slowly and calmly; women carry baskets on their heads along tiny paths up and down the hills. There are no tractors; the hills are too steep. It is typical of the landscape of Nepal; unlike most developing countries, 90% of the population live in villages and most work in agriculture.

The modern world still invades the serenity of rural Nepal in a furtive and insidious manner. The borders to the south are huge and open, and labour migration, trade and tourism strengthen the links with India. The trafficking of young girls for the sex trade is common; it is estimated that

up to 200,000 girls and women are working in the brothels and red light districts of Indian cities at any one time. Fulmaya's story is typical in that girls are often promised work in something that sounds innocuous, but which is in fact a front for suppliers of the sex trade. When girls like Fulmaya return to Nepal, many are HIV positive and often suffering from other health problems, as well as the psychological trauma which results from their experiences. The taboos against discussing sex create further problems, especially for children.

The Suryamukhi Girls' Group helps girls who have been in Indian brothels and other exploitative situations to deal with problems such as AIDS and to get back on their feet again. They learn skills to earn a living – such as tailoring and goat farming – and they also gain confidence. They learn not to be deceived again, they earn respect from their families and they learn to deal with the prejudice they often encounter in their local communities. Fulmaya went on to train as a cook in a well-known hotel, and later became head cook at a local skills development centre.

Chakkali Bal, another girl who was helped by the Suryamukhi Girls' Group, actively works in the community to change people's attitudes towards HIV. Her story is even more horrific than Fulmaya's. At the age of fifteen, she was trafficked to an Indian brothel by her brother-in-law. Thinking she was going to see her sister-in-law, who in fact did not exist, she found herself in a big market near the local train station, and was then dragged into a brothel:

"A blackish man with long moustache came and asked [me] to lie down in the bed but I refused and cried loudly but he rudely beat me and pushed with glowing cigarette in the chest and neck. I could not tolerate for long and finally surrendered to him. Then started my living in hell by satisfying to many clients. Some of them were cruel and rascals and beat me for not sucking his penis. In fact I live in that hell for four years.

"I was rescued from the brothel by the help of local police in Bombay and they helped me to return to Nepal with a rescue team from Nepal. The people who rescued me from the brothel helped me to reach my home. After two months, I was suffered from various illness and severe fever and diarrhoea. In Kathmandu, I was tested blood and found as HIV positive. At that time I actually didn't know what HIV/AIDS was. Many people said me that I got HIV and they started to hate me.

"During that time GWP staff contacted me and they provided support for medicines and helped me to educate on HIV/AIDS. It was nine years before when GWP staff came to me and supported me to settle me in the family and in the community. Community people started to say me as a *Bombaiya* [girls who return from brothels in Bombay] ... It was really disappointing to hear such words from the neighbours who used to love me as a lovely girl of Basamadhi."

It's a terrible indictment that this kind of situation is so common that there is a special word for girls who return to their homes after suffering such a fate.

On the positive side, is it not inspiring to think that our purchases of fair trade products – like the gift-wrap made by GET Paper – are used to benefit girls like Fulmaya and Chakkali? Fair trade does not just provide people with decent wages and living conditions. In many cases, all around the world, fair trade organisations campaign against injustice and exploitation, and help individuals like these girls to get back on their feet again after they have been through horrific experiences. After receiving help from GWP, Chakkali moved on to help and support others, as she explains:

"Since last seven years I'm a paid peer educator of GWP working against HIV/AIDS and communicate against girls' trafficking too. Now I feel myself very empowered for that I got marry with my love Mr Sukra. Although people did not accept him as my husband and said that PLHA [people living with HIV/AIDS] cannot marry with a healthy guy. But at last, people accepted us as happy couple with HIV. I'm fully empowered and could express my feeling in front of many people of media and foreigners."

Chakkali has put a lot of time and effort into educating people about the problems of child trafficking and HIV/AIDS; she has helped to change people's attitudes and perhaps, as a result of her work, a few children have escaped the hell that she went through.

It was in September 2006 that I received the email from Asha Handicrafts. It was not about shipments, prices, product design or any

of the usual subjects. I had already visited one of Tara's slum schools and met former schoolchildren at Karm Marg. I had discovered how – through poverty and desperation – some families sell their children into virtual slavery. Now I was given a wonderful opportunity to do something myself. It was to raise funds, through the annual Mumbai marathon, to help struggling parents to send their children to school.

"We are planning to get a group of International Volunteers to join us to run for fair trade in the Mumbai Marathon," the email read. The Mumbai Marathon Team "will be an exciting, vibrating and enthusiastic group of colour and noise taking the message of fair trade to the streets of Mumbai."

Over a hundred people from Asha would be taking part, and the money raised would be used for their educational programme. Would I like to join them? The Mumbai Marathon, the email continued, is one of the largest in the world, attracting international athletes, a host of celebrities and wide media coverage. Thirty thousand people take part every year.

I wasn't sure about the athletes and the media coverage. A picture of me struggling along beside any kind of athlete would be the last thing I would want to see in the papers; but I enjoy a challenge, and the idea of helping unfortunate children appealed. The email had arrived not long after I had visited GET Paper in Nepal. The stories of girls like Fulmaya and Chakkali were on my mind.

"OK, yes," I replied, without thinking. "I'll do it." The button was clicked; the message was sent. It was too late to retract.

Acting on impulse can be dangerous, and it didn't take long before the cool light of day started dawning in my mind. "I'm 53 years old," I thought. "I used to come last in cross-country at school. I'm not a runner and I'm not fit."

I started to panic and phoned a friend.

"A marathon?" he said. "You must be crazy! You'll need a year to get in training! How long have you got?"

"Three or four months," I replied.

"Well, that settles it. You can't train for a marathon in that time. Can't you think of something else to do that's just as challenging? Why don't you open another shop or cycle to Paris or something?"

By this stage my mind was set on the marathon, however; I had

committed myself to it and didn't want to retract. Fortunately a compromise was possible. A half marathon – thirteen miles – was more achievable, but would still be a hefty challenge.

I set out that evening down a local footpath to see how well I could fare. The weather was wet and miserable; the tree branches dripped with rain, and the path was lined with weeds and dirty brambles. Apparently, you can become quite addicted to running; but it must be difficult in weather like this. The excitement, colour and enthusiasm promised by Asha would, I suspected, be at the end of the marathon, not in the weeks ahead. I plodded on, wondering what on earth I was doing.

As my legs grew more weary, my mind became more active, and images of some of the children I had seen in India started coming back to me. I remembered a modern hotel near Mumbai Airport, with its own vast shopping mall; its shops sold clothes, jewellery and gifts as fashionable and expensive as anything you could find in Paris or London. It was evening, and the bright lighting inside contrasted with the gloom without. The revolving doors of the entrance were flanked by two doorkeepers with enormous moustaches, dressed in costumes from the days of the Raj. Not fifty yards away, in the chaos of the building site around the newly built hotel, were three large concrete sewage pipes, grey and dusty. Inside them, a bare-footed girl of about seven and her two younger brothers were settling down for the night. The contrast of light and dark, rich and poor, could not have been more clearly stated. It was for children like these that I would be running in the marathon.

To my surprise, I managed to keep running for nearly an hour – about four miles. I arrived back home exhausted but elated. If I could increase this distance by a mile each week, I would be able to manage the half marathon in January.

September turned into October, and gradually the running became easier. I ran down by the River Ouse, which runs through the centre of York, looking out for the kingfishers which sometimes fly along its banks. Rowers from St Peter's School would shoot by, and I would pass other joggers, feeling like one of them, instead of like an amateur who didn't know what he was doing. On some days the sun came out, lifting the spirits.

One evening in late October I ran up to the campus of York University

at Heslington and around its lake. Thirty-five years before, I had been a student there myself, and it was a strange feeling running along those covered ways that I knew so well, and imagining myself back in a distant time when the future seemed so open, the world so unexplored. I passed Goodricke College and saw the room in which I had lived as an eighteen-year old; who was living there now? As I turned round the end of the lake at Derwent College and started heading for home, I felt immensely pleased – by the time I got back, I would have run seven miles, my best distance yet.

Then came a setback. On my next run, sharp pains started shooting through my right foot, and then my hip-joint. I had to slow down, and by mid-November, give up running almost completely. I staggered along to see Dr Ashley – who was as friendly as ever, but unable to help.

"These things often happen when you run," he said, "it's nothing you need to worry about. Just stop for a few weeks and you'll be ok."

"But I'm running a half marathon in January," I told him. "I can't wait a few weeks. I have to get into training now!"

"I'm sorry, but I think you've come to the wrong place," he replied, raising his eyebrows. "It sounds like you need to see a psychiatrist."

Giving up was not an option. I had to keep at it. But after a couple of short runs, the pains got even worse, and soon, it was painful to run at all. I was forced to follow doctor's advice, and rest. I phoned my friend again, and told him the furthest I'd run so far was seven miles.

"You'll just have to rest completely," he said. "Then when the day comes, run as far as you can, and walk the rest of the way. I'm sure you won't be the only one."

The days passed in an agony of anticipation. Would I be able to run? Finally, on the 18th of January, the journey to India began. I set off with Sarah, one of Shared Earth's designers, who was also taking part in the marathon. A delay of fifteen hours at Dubai Airport was not a good omen. It meant we'd be running the day after arriving, and would not have recovered from jet lag.

The marathon was almost upon us. Sarah, more astute than I, had discovered that the Asha runners were going on the 'Fun Run', an alternative option of about four miles. She jumped at this opportunity and agreed to join them. But I'd already been sponsored by several

of Shared Earth's suppliers, as well as a large number of friends and relatives.

"I'm entering the Mumbai marathon," I said, "will you sponsor me?"

"Wow, that's amazing!" was the usual response.

"Well, it's not the full marathon, it's only half," I explained; it was best to be honest about such things from the start. They were still impressed; but to qualify this further and to phone up my sponsors and say, "actually, I'm only running four miles now" would be too much of a let-down. And what about the uncle who had told me he was not giving me a donation, but sponsoring me by the mile? And the friend who was so impressed – or perhaps just didn't think I would make it – that he promised to double his sponsorship if I reached the finishing line? I decided I would do my utmost to run the half marathon, whatever it took.

Our hosts from Asha greeted us at Mumbai Airport with wide smiles, and guided us through the cries of "taxi, taxi, you want taxi?" and "hotel, hotel, you want hotel?" There was a cool breeze, and the scent of India, a mixture of rich vegetation, spices, dust, and from time to time less pleasant substances, welcomed us. It was late at night, the streets were as quiet as they get in a busy Indian city, and it wasn't long before we arrived at our guesthouse in the suburbs. We collapsed thankfully on our beds, with that wonderful feeling you get when you put your suitcase down in your room at last, at the end of a long and difficult journey. You can relax. The problems behind were over, and the challenges ahead were still to come. We made the most of what was left of the night to grab a few hours sleep.

Next morning, we attended a marathon workshop for Asha's runners, where we met six people from Ten Thousand Villages, a fair trade retailer in Canada, who were also taking part. The day was tinged with anxiety.

Finally, the day I had been dreading arrived: 21st January, 2007. I got out of bed with trepidation. Prasad, an unassuming youth who worked in Asha's warehouse, arrived to collect us. His tousled black hair and ready smile seemed to indicate that life was for living, not for worrying about, and I felt reassured as he escorted us on foot to the local train station. It was 5.30 in the morning. Apart from a few rickshaw drivers and street-sellers, still fast asleep in their vehicles or by the side of the road, the streets were almost deserted.

The station was busier, and so was the train. Both were filled with young Indian men, clearly bound for the same destination as ourselves, and all of them were in high spirits, laughing and joking as if they were children at the start of an exciting school trip. They all looked incredibly fit and healthy, and they seemed to have enormous energy, as if they really were young children. I was beginning to feel very out of place; how did I manage to let myself in for this? But it was too late to turn back. I tried to smile and think positive. "How about that guy down the aisle?" I thought. "He doesn't look quite so self-assured. He looks almost my age, too; perhaps I'm not as alone as I thought." But if he was apprehensive, it wasn't about the marathon. I was about to approach him when the train stopped, and he got out, two stops too soon.

At last we reached the station, and joined the throngs of people making their way to the huge field (or 'maidan') where the marathon was to start. It was still early in the day, crisp and cool, but the field, with its dusty grass and patches of dry brown earth, hinted at the heat to come. It was dotted about as far as the eye could see with groups of people, most of them chatting and getting ready for the marathon. Almost all were men, and almost all were Indians, with just an occasional runner from some other nationality to be seen here or there. They weren't all young; occasionally older men could be spotted amongst the crowd. The laughter and joking we had seen on the train had given way to looks of resolution and thoughtfulness; there was an air of seriousness everywhere. This was the real thing.

The six Canadians, who had stayed in a different hotel, appeared. Four were women and they were in good spirits; they were taking part in the Fun Run and had a couple of hours to wait. Ron and Luke were father and son, supporting each other, and they were the only ones in the Asha contingent who were attempting the half marathon with me. They were lanky, cheerful and assured, and they looked as if they knew what they were doing. I latched on to them and tried, without appearing too unconfident, to reveal some of my anxieties. Ron was an old hand, and had run marathons before.

"Every twenty or thirty minutes," he suggested, "stop and walk for a minute, to recover a bit." This was valuable advice.

There was no time for a real conversation; before long we were making

our way to the starting line. It wasn't really a line. There were no pistols going off, officials telling you what to do, or assistants ticking names off on clipboards, just hundreds of people milling around and then gradually starting to run. It was all gloriously anarchic. As we reached the area where walking turned to running, I was hoping I would be able to accompany Ron and Luke, to get some moral support on the way. This was not to be. They quickly forged ahead – the last I saw of them until after the event. It was 7am.

Soon, however, I realised I didn't need support. I was running, I was on my own and that was fine. I suddenly became aware that there were people I was actually overtaking! Some of them even looked young and fit and healthy. I must have something in me after all. I wasn't concerned about beating anyone; my aim was to run for as long as possible and somehow reach the finishing line, running, walking or crawling. But it was a good feeling to see that I had started off well, with no sign yet of my injuries recurring. If this continued, at least I would not come last, as I used to do in cross-country at school.

A young couple with British Airways T-shirts passed me. "Can't have this," I thought. But my short-lived attempt to catch them up was unsuccessful. They disappeared into the distance. Then another person passed me. He was wearing a T-shirt with the logo of a multinational business. I lost sight of him, until a few minutes later, there he was again, running beside me. "I can't be doing too badly," I thought. "I must have overtaken him and now he's caught up again." This happened several times. I was getting almost fond of him; evidently I wasn't doing too badly. It was like Shared Earth keeping up with Marks and Sparks. Then suddenly it was a woman. I realised they'd all been different people, wearing the same corporate T–shirt.

The tables where assistants handed out bottles of water were a great source of encouragement. Every time I passed one I realised I'd run a significant distance further. As I drank or poured the water over my head, and threw the bottle to the side of the road, I thought of the environment and plastic bottle mountains, and resolved to pick up a few bottles in the street when I got back to England, and recycle them, to make up for this infraction of my principles.

Runners started passing on the other side of the road, real athletes,

including two or three Africans. They looked as if they were sprinting; how could they possibly keep up that pace for mile after mile? And was I really taking part in the same event as them? It seemed unbelievable. I envied them; apart from their obvious fitness, they were on their way back. People on the side-walks clapped and cheered as they went past. I pretended the cheers were for me, and took heart.

I was immensely pleased that I was still running; there was still no sign of serious pain reoccurring. A placard appeared by the side of the road: 9km. Brilliant, I thought – I've reached half way! Then six or seven minutes later: 10km. I felt I was making really good progress. Suddenly, another sign: HALF WAY. Is this some kind of mistake? I thought. Or a sick joke? I asked a fellow runner.

"No, no, marathon is 42 kilometre, half marathon 21 kilometre," he informed me. I was used to thinking in miles and hadn't got the conversion right. I had thought that a half marathon was 18 kilometres.

From that brutal moment it was a question of keeping going. It was winter in India, and when we set off, the weather was pleasantly cool; now it was beginning to heat up. Fortunately much of the route, which was on a wide road on the seafront, was shaded by tall buildings, which helped. And I was still running!

I'd come so far now that it would be awful to give up. My legs were aching, but my mind was clear. I thought about the generosity of the people who'd sponsored me, and about the children who would benefit from the money raised. One by one the refreshment tables and mileage points passed by.

Finally, a long, dark tree-lined avenue – I was nearly at the end! The avenue seemed to go on and on. But eventually, I was there, and the marathon was over. Like the start line, it wasn't quite clear exactly where the finishing line was, but people were slowing down and stopping, and I wearily but gladly joined them. What an amazing feeling! No doubt the looks of exhaustion, pride and happiness that I saw on other runners' faces were reflected in my own. It had taken nearly two and a half hours, and felt like twice that. But the time was irrelevant; my real source of joy was to have completed the race at all, and especially to have run all the way. It really seemed like a miracle. I wanted my PE teacher from school to be there; those awful cross-country runs at school were only

short, but I'd always struggled to finish them. Now, at the age of 53, I'd run thirteen miles.

Like a racehorse after a race, I walked around to avoid getting cramp. Meanwhile, huge crowds of people were gathering nearby, all heading in the same direction, and I realised that the Fun Run was about to start. I stood on a low wall hoping to spot the rest of the Asha contingent, both to wave good luck and also to show that I'd made it back myself. So many thousands of people were taking part that I almost despaired of seeing them. Asha, however, had provided us all with bright red T-shirts, printed with the words 'Fair Trade – Small Change, Big Difference.' I was about to give up when I spotted a large patch of red amongst the crowd, and Sarah waving. Lots of smiles and laughter, and then they were gone.

Later, I found they'd had to walk the whole way; the crowd had been so thick that running had been impossible. I was enormously pleased that I'd opted for the half marathon, and hadn't backed down despite my injuries. It wasn't just that it raised a lot of money for families who couldn't afford to send their children to school. It had also been an amazing personal challenge. It gave me renewed self-confidence and showed me that if you really want something and are prepared to go for it, almost anything is possible in life. In fact, probably without that new self-confidence, this book that you are reading would never have been started.

So I have benefited as much as the children for whom I was running. And that's one of the things about fair trade. We're not just 'helping the poor' when we buy fair trade products. We gain ourselves, in all sorts of ways that we may not fully understand at the time.

The field where the race ended was dotted with tents, refreshment stalls, groups of supporters, and a growing band of runners who had completed the marathon. I was so delighted at completing the course that I was inspired by a new energy. You could sense that we all wanted to enjoy ourselves and savour the atmosphere before we made our way back to our homes and hotels. There was a camaraderie amongst us as we wandered around, listening to bands playing, buying drinks and snacks, and chatting to fellow runners. Strangers were now friends; good-feeling was in the air.

An elderly Sikh approached me. His white hair and beard could not disguise the deep lines on his face and forehead. They suggested suffering and struggle, but he also had an air of calm and wisdom, as if these experiences had helped him to grow, instead of leading to bitterness or despair. His eyes smiled as he walked towards me.

He was a small man and his knees looked incongruous as they stuck out below his shorts. His loose shirt was an off-white colour – it had clearly been worn many times – and his turban was sweaty and grimy. In fact, he was as unlike the athletic youths I had seen on the train as it's possible to imagine. Nodding for emphasis, he told me he too had just completed the half marathon. His steady smile showed his satisfaction at being able to make this simple statement, and the special way in which he was looking at me was overpowering. There seemed to be a tangible goodness that was coming out of nowhere. Although we were silent, we might both have been thinking and feeling the same as each other: "I may look old, but what does age matter? I have conquered! I have run before and I will run again! I will never give up!"

I thought of some of the Indian men and women I'd seen, their expressions of hope, determination, acceptance, sorrow, and occasionally despair. I thought of the laughter of children, and the reason I keep coming to India each year, to buy from producers using the principles of fair trade, to repay some of the kindness I was shown on my first visit there when I was only eighteen. It seemed so easy for me, a well-off member of a well-off society, to make glib statements about 'helping people to improve their lives.' I wondered what this Sikh would think of it all.

I wondered whether to talk to him about fair trade, to explain the logo on my T-shirt, 'Run for Fair Trade.' It's a serious topic that means a lot to me, but I know there's a danger of sermonising about it as people aren't always ready to hear about something which may be a strange or challenging concept. But his smiling eyes seemed to reassure me that I needn't say anything; the logo on my T-shirt said it all. It felt as if he was reading my thoughts, and he already knew what I was about to say, that caring for others starts not with governments and corporations, but with each individual in his or her own heart.

"You like energy food?" he asked enquiringly, as if it was the most

natural thing in the world to ask a perfect stranger. We were standing next to a large white tent and the sun was getting hotter and hotter as the morning advanced. The cool breeze of earlier had died out completely. He brought out a small bag of dates from a pocket on his running shorts. "Very good energy food," he said.

They were more delicious than the most expensive dates I have ever eaten on Christmas Day. As we ate together, we talked about our experiences, as if we were old friends who hadn't seen each other for years. It wasn't long before he was reaching into another pocket. A card appeared, with details of his address in New Delhi. What else would one carry when running a marathon? He gave one to me.

"Next time you come to Delhi, you stay with me," he said, nodding significantly as if to show he really meant it. "No problem – you stay with me." I thought of all the tourists I saw in my home town of York, and compared the way I acted towards them with the hospitality of this elderly Sikh. The comparison was not in my favour.

Asha Handicrafts wanted the Mumbai marathon to make 'a big noise for fair trade' – and it did. Fair trade is well known in most developed countries; almost everyone in Britain now recognises the Fairtrade logo. But in developing countries, it's largely an unknown concept. To attract attention, we all wore ribbons or headbands with the phrase 'Run for Fair Trade', had our faces painted with red and white lines, and wore red T-shirts. Some of us even carried placards and banners. The fair trade story was carried in major newspapers in India and broadcast on several TV channels. Hundreds of young people, a few celebrities and several commercial companies became involved in the fair trade movement as a result.

The marathon was also a great fund-raising success, raising over £12,000 for Asha's educational programs. Although the Indian government provides free education, many artisans struggle to make a living, and can't afford to pay for 'extras', such as books, uniforms and travel to and from school. And when there's not enough food on the

table, the idea that your children can contribute to the family income is a tempting one.

Children are not uncommonly sold off to pay debts or ward off destitution – or simply sent out to work. That's one of the reasons why child labour is still so predominant in the world today.

Two-thirds of the money Asha raised was from Shared Earth – a fantastic tribute to all the friends, relatives, suppliers and customers throughout the UK who supported us! The programme provides small grants to artisans who are in difficulty, minimising the risk of child exploitation and helping to protect children like Fulmaya and Chakkali.

One beneficiary was Suman Prajapati, a young widow from a small village near Jaipur. Due to her large and poor family, she was married at the age of thirteen and had her first child at the age of sixteen. Her husband recently died of a heart attack. Suman – whose education ended when she married – was 31. With no skills or qualifications herself, she was desperate that her own three children should do better in life.

She started to rebuild her life with courage and determination, joining Asha's Toy Library Project as an assistant teacher, helping to provide non-formal education to artisans' children. Today, she is earning and able to sustain her children, all of whom – with a small grant from the Educational Fund – are at school.

"I had a dream," she said, "that I would provide my children with quality education and create a better future for them, but after my husband's death I had lost all hope. Now, with support from Asha, I am sure that my dream will come true."

15 Fair Trade Sex Toys

FAIR TRADE SEX toys?? You've got to be joking! Well, I was when I first came up with the idea. It was 2004 and I was visiting People Tree in New Delhi. The name People Tree is best known as a fair trade clothing business, based in Japan and with a branch in London. Its founder, Safia Minney, makes extraordinary efforts to ensure its clothing comes from fair trade sources throughout the supply chain. However, there's another People Tree which most people haven't heard about. It was set up at an earlier date by Gurpreet Sidhu in Connaught Place, New Delhi in 1990. It is still a successful, thriving fair trade shop today. It caters largely to tourists, selling T-shirts, handmade paper, fair trade gifts and, in a cramped rear room, books on global politics and development.

I was visiting Gurpreet with Itxaso, our head designer, to see if we could work together in any way. There were no stairs; to reach the office above the shop we had to climb a rickety ladder through a hole in the ceiling, as if we were climbing on deck from the hold of a ship. We had already spent several hours that morning with another supplier, and I was tired. It was a hot day and the added exertion of this climb, balancing my bags precariously as I ascended, made me sweaty. I sat down on a floor cushion, longing for a drink.

Gurpreet is a feminist. She's the kind of person you're not immediately at ease with – at least if you're a man. You worry that you're going to say the wrong thing. This was the first time I had met her and I didn't want to cause offence. I decided to leave most of the talking to Itxaso as

I thought she would do a better job than I would. Would any of People Tree's products be suitable for Shared Earth? A long discussion about textiles followed. Then the topic of recycling came up – and she asked me for ideas.

I have long been keen on recycling, and despite being tired was eager to get on my hobbyhorse once more. Had Gurpreet heard of our UK supplier Cutouts, which makes excellent desk and table accessories from circuit boards, coffee cups, yoghurt pots, old CDs and rubber tyres? The circuit board products were particularly unusual, I suggested.

At the mention of rubber tyres Gurpreet's ears instantly pricked up. "Rubber tyres?" she said. "Wonderful! One of our most needy suppliers has loads of them, and they don't know what to do with them. They would love to work with you – I'll get in touch with them straight away!"

I realised I had made a mistake. Apart from anything else, the products made from rubber tyres – mouse mats and coasters – had been the least popular in the whole of the Cutouts range. I tried to tell Gurpreet this, but it was too late. This was not an obstacle as far as she was concerned. She was concerned about producers – not about sales.

This is not uncommon. Sometimes aspiring producer groups send me long emails about what a great job they are doing – providing excellent wages, improving conditions, building schools and so on. Are you interested in supporting this wonderful fair trade project by placing an order? they ask. They're so enthusiastic about the 'fairness' of their project that they forget all about the 'trade' – and fail to mention what it is they're trying to sell.

I tried to put Gurpreet off without appearing rude. It's always difficult when people think they have a brilliant product and you know it's not going to sell in your market. You want to be open and honest and tell them so, but at the same time you don't want to upset them. You feel especially guilty if they're poor and desperate for work. Will their children be starving or sent out to work long hours because of their situation? Could you avert this by placing just a tiny order, even if the products never sell? You have to remind yourself that fair trade is about trade, not charity. That's its strength and the reason it will continue to grow.

"I don't think rubber is quite the right material for desk accessories,"

I said. "Its texture is a bit off-putting. It's too rough." In fact, just the thought of rubber tyres was making me feel hot. For some reason, I kept thinking of lorries crossing dry and sandy deserts. How long would it be before I could go back to my guesthouse, turn on the fan and have a cool drink? Then I felt guilty. How could I be so self-centred when so many people in India and other Third World countries don't have a decent electricity supply, or even access to clean water?

"I still think this could be a great opportunity," continued Gurpreet, who was clearly reluctant to give up. "We have all this rubber, surely some use could be found for it? If desk accessories won't work, can you think of something else?"

I racked my brains, but my fuddled mind wasn't working properly. I looked to Itxaso for inspiration. She smiled encouragingly, mumbled and said she couldn't think of anything.

"You must be able to think of something, surely," said Gurpreet. But we couldn't. It had been a long day and I was tired. I was getting more and more tired as every minute passed.

So the words just popped out of my mouth.

"How about fair trade sex toys?"

Gurpreet, who had been talking almost non-stop since we arrived, was suddenly speechless. Men, honestly! They're all the same! What a stupid, senseless joke! She began to frown, then burst into giggles.

The conversation moved on to other subjects, but you could tell the idea of fair trade sex toys had caught Gurpreet's imagination and could not easily be suppressed. For the rest of our meeting, she kept putting her hand to her mouth to stop herself giggling again.

My suggestion was only made in jest, but the idea of fair trade sex toys is not as far-fetched as you might think. I recently discovered that a Brighton-based company, Fair Deal Trading, has for many years been developing fair trade sports balls and trainers, made from FSC-certified rubber. They've developed balloons with the same material and, as a logical next step, have just introduced a range of fair trade condoms. A fair trade condom, they claim, "offers our customers the opportunity of making love with an eye on fair play."

And if the idea of fair trade sex toys seemed absurd to you when you started reading this book – as it did to me when I started writing

it – imagine my surprise and prepare yourself for a shock. A German company has just launched a fair trade vibrator made with latex from Fair Deal Trading's suppliers in Sri Lanka. It's not a joke, it's genuine and it's already changing people's lives. Not only has the Forest Stewardship Council certified that the trees are being sustainably planted and managed, but the rubber tappers receive a social premium on top of the normal price. They use this for health and welfare projects, and toilets and a well have already been built.

One thing is clear: fair trade is changing; it has gone through a metamorphosis since the mid-nineties. Traidcraft, the UK's largest fair trader, illustrates the change that has taken place. Its beginnings were in handicrafts and it relied for custom on fair trade enthusiasts. Since the mid-nineties, its policy has been transformed and its turnover has trebled. To its traditional customers, it gradually added businesses which stock fair trade products in bulk because they see it as a consumer trend which will increase their profits.

'Mainstreaming', as it is known, is more advanced in the UK than anywhere else in the world, and refers to the efforts of companies like Traidcraft and Green & Black's to promote fair trade products to commercial customers as well as to those who already strongly support fair trade.

A few people – especially in Europe – argue that the whole trading system, because it is based on profit, will always exploit the poor. The supermarkets, they say, are only doing it to make money. Stocking a few fair trade products, they claim, is just a token gesture, aimed in the end just at making more profit.

Do the supermarkets have any commitment to fairness for its own sake? Their basic commitment, it's true, is to supplying what their customers want and to making more profit for their shareholders.

Sometimes, large companies try to 'greenwash' their image by promoting an ethical product or service in order to divert attention away from their more dubious policies elsewhere. Nestlé was criticised for many years for its ethics. It then launched its own-brand fair trade coffee.

In itself, this was an excellent step forward, but some people saw it as a cynical exercise in self-promotion, especially when they discovered the amount of money Nestlé was spending on marketing this one product.

Despite these worries, I'm in favour of mainstreaming. If commercial retailers are not involved then the fair trade movement will remain a niche market benefiting only a small number of producers. The growth in trade which comes with mainstreaming maximises the impact fair trade has on poverty, affecting far more people than would otherwise be the case. As Paul Chandler, Director of Traidcraft, points out, "we need our traditional base of fair trade activists, but now we also need the skills and clout and financial resources of commercial partners to make fair trade really grow."

Simple decisions may affect the lives of thousands. In one of the boldest fair trade moves ever, Tate & Lyle have recently announced their intention to convert all of their retail sugar to fair trade, multiplying by tenfold the amount of fair trade sugar sold in the UK. Tens of thousands of small-scale growers in Belize are expected to benefit. Nestlé's own-brand coffee and Sainsbury's decision to convert all its bananas to fair trade are other examples.

I believe fair trade is an idea whose time has come. 'Unfair' trade succeeds because its effects are hidden from us. The fair trade movement tells us about what is really happening – how children work in sweatshops to make our clothes, for instance – and provides us with alternatives. Our consciences are aroused. It's like the global movement against slavery in the nineteenth century. Slavery is now unacceptable; a total attitude transformation has taken place. Is a similar transformation under way at present, on the issue of global trade?

The more fair trade products that sell, the more the ideas of fair trade take root. But it's not going to happen overnight. You have to start somewhere – and this includes Nestlé. The supermarkets are not static, they are changing. Competition makes them innovative and adaptable. Their customers are vital to them, and if enough of us want them to be more ethical, they will become more ethical. Some commercial buyers are already personally committed to fair trade. More and more young people – the future employees, managers and even directors of our large companies and supermarkets – are in favour of fair trade. As these

people move up the ladder, the influence they exert will increase, and the pressure for change will grow. Fair trade is not a fashion, it's a long term trend!

Fair trade works from the bottom up. That's its strength. We're making a better world by the way we shop, bit by bit. Some people say it's just softening the edges of an unfair system, but we have to start somewhere. The most important thing is to abolish the worst excesses of poverty, like the farmers who are paid less for their crops than they cost to produce. That's what fair trade is trying to do. In doing so, it's making us think about where our goods come from, and making us aware that trade is about people, not just about goods or money or profit. Is it idealistic to hope that the next step will be legislation to support the voluntary initiatives of forward-looking companies, to ensure that ethical practices are applied by all?

What are the limits to fair trade? If William Wainman can start a successful business selling coffins, why shouldn't someone else do the same for garden furniture or shop-fittings? And what about mass-produced products like cars, computers and plastic buckets?

"Fair trade is about human labour," comments James Lloyd of Fair Deal Trading. "If human labour is involved, you can have a fair trade element. If you can have fair trade tea, why not fair trade T-shirts, or fair trade computers for that matter? The supply chain will be harder to manage; computers contain a lot of different metals. But the mining of the metals can be made more ethical. The principle – treating producers fairly – is the same."

We already have the beginnings of fair trade tourism, banking and IT. What about other services like transport and freight, property and construction, even insurance? There are huge opportunities for fair trade and more and more fair trade businesses are being set up. We already have fair trade coffins and condoms!

One of the most positive developments in fair trade at the moment is the willingness of the Fairtrade Foundation (and hopefully of its parent body FLO) to explore new areas. Traditionally, it has concentrated on

food, but this may not always be the case. Harriet Lamb, its executive director, sees great opportunities for the future.

"We can't do everything, and there's still enormous scope in food – we've just obtained agreements on olive oil, pulses and a selection of fresh fruit and vegetables, for instance. Agricultural food commodities still have to be our main priority. But we're looking at other products too, like jute, silk and rubber, even at things like wood and the mining industry. A key principle will be to collaborate with experts in the field. For instance we're working with the Marine Stewardship Council on prawns, and we see a lot of opportunities to work with the Forest Stewardship Council on wood. We also want to work with IFAT on crafts."

The mainstreaming of fair trade in the last 10-15 years has led to an upsurge in food sales, whilst handicraft sales have remained static. So the above, if the Fairtrade Foundation carries it through, is indeed good news. Its Fairtrade label is well recognised by the public. A new label from a different fair trade organisation would stand less chance of success in attracting large orders, and would also be confusing for consumers.

★↗★

How have fair trade shops coped with the mainstreaming of fair trade, and the competition which it represents? In some cases their response has been similar to that of the radical bookshops to increased competition from chains like Waterstone's in the 1980s. They still sell similar products and find it hard to innovate and adapt to changing times.

One thing that will never change, unfortunately, is that small shops will find it almost impossible to compete with the supermarkets, either on price or on convenience, if they sell the same products.

However, there's a wealth of new and exciting crafts appearing each year. Sometimes, fair trade shops can even beat the high street chains on price, and for uniqueness we will always be ahead of the game. "It's the traders who import shed-loads of rubbish from China," says Les Harper of Siesta, "who will suffer most. If we keep selling original, interesting products, we will be ok."

How is Shared Earth coping? Recession is obviously worrying. Early in 2008, I attended a property auction; our shop in Liverpool was coming under the hammer – the building, that is, not our business. The only danger for us was that we might exchange our landlord for a difficult one. My recycled shopper looked out of place amongst all the briefcases.

"Who will start me off at £1 million? £800,000? £700,000? Thank you, sir, £700,000." It was an interesting experience, but it wasn't me bidding. How many people bid too much?

Property values may be shrinking, but I am confident that fair trade is growing; and Shared Earth seems to have a formula which works. In the last two years, we have increased from five to eight shops, including one in Stratford-upon-Avon in November 2008. I am proud of our achievements; we have an excellent management team and hard-working staff, from the sales assistants in our shops to everyone in our office. There's not a company I know which has more committed employees.

Our efforts are concentrating now on seeing us through a difficult economic time. But it would be a mistake to stand still. If anything is growing faster than support for fair trade, it's concern about the environment. My next ambition is to open an 'eco' shop, combining fair trade products, especially those made from recycled materials, with energy-saving devices, ecological household accessories and the like. Most of Shared Earth's products are already made from sustainable or recycled materials, but the environment is a number one priority, and I want to go a step further.

How have fair traders changed their attitudes towards the environment over the last few years? Twenty years ago a customer came into the One World Shop in Edinburgh and complained about their recycled writing sets. Traidcraft had always carried a wide selection and distributed them to many fair trade shops at the time. She thought they were out of place.

"This is a *Third World* shop," she complained. "If you keep pushing these things you'll damage my commitment to you."

Such a response would be unlikely today; we're beginning to see how closely the problems of poverty and the environment are linked. Fair trade can be both part of the problem and part of the solution.

As fair trade importers and consumers, we're getting better all the time

at making demands of our suppliers. We have good reason to question producers about their practices, because environmental legislation is generally more stringent and more strictly enforced in the First World than in the Third. However, the problems we face with the environment today are largely caused by over-consumption, and that's our responsibility. Both the environmental and financial cost of the products we buy should be taken into account – and we should be paying for it.

"I saw something on the local news the other day," Richard Adams told me recently, "a village in Bangladesh that I visited before I founded Traidcraft in 1979. It was marvellous; the villagers had permanent buildings instead of mud huts and clearly there had been terrific changes in people's lives. A whole community had been transformed through fair trade. It was on a small scale, but you could see that fair trade really works."

But will all the successes and benefits brought by fair trade be cancelled out by environmental disasters?

Andy Atkins, Director of Friends of the Earth, is distinctly worried. I asked him if environmental problems like soil erosion, deforestation and global warming were likely in the future to increase poverty more than unfair trade. His answer was instant.

"They already are," he said, "There's no doubt about it. Climate change will reduce growing seasons, and land that was marginal for growing crops may no longer be viable at all. Water is the most important issue of all. Climate change affects rainfall patterns – there's either too much or too little. This results in either floods or drought; intense rainfall leads to soil erosion too, making it even more difficult in following years to grow crops."

Radical new thinking is needed by the fair trade movement. The early fair trade pioneers wanted to do more than just contribute to famine and disaster relief; by campaigning for fairer trade, they wanted to solve the underlying causes of poverty itself. And they didn't just want to campaign. By distributing products like fair trade coffee, they avoided political lobbying and bridged the gap between producers and consumers, giving us something practical to do to help. Since then many millions of people throughout the world have escaped from poverty as a result of fair trade.

Things have changed, however, and the world has moved on. The causes of poverty are different now and are likely to be even more so in another thirty years' time. Environmental problems could outweigh all the benefits fair trade has brought, even if it grows to a hundred times its size.

The basic problem is that the natural resources of the world – oil, minerals, water, land and so on – are limited, and we are already in deficit; we are using up more of them than we can replace or sustain. The world population is rising, and as countries like China and India develop, the pressure on resources grows even more.

I have already mentioned how China, with its huge population, is consuming more meat as its standard of living rises. It is also buying more of the world's minerals to feed its industries. In the last two years, the world price of silver has doubled due largely to Chinese orders. The price rises have led to a slump in demand, and as a result thousands of silversmiths in countries like India and Peru have lost their jobs. Shared Earth has been forced into cutting back its orders drastically, whilst Oxfam has stopped ordering silver jewellery completely for the first time in many years.

Land is a key resource, and there's not enough of it either. Whether it's used to rear more meat or to grow crops for biofuels doesn't make much difference. Either way, more land is needed than is available, so the price of food goes up. It's the poor who suffer most – and unfair trade is not the reason.

Resources like oil and minerals are non-renewable. However, renewable resources such as forests and seafood from the oceans are also suffering and are often being harvested in an unsustainable manner. That's why it's excellent that the Fairtrade Foundation, in developing fair trade prawns and wood, wants to work closely with the Marine and Forest Stewardship Councils.

★★★

Are specific resources under threat for any of Shared Earth's producers, and is anything being done about it? One thing we sell a lot of is woodcarvings, and, like almost all fair traders, we try to import

softwoods instead of hardwoods. Yet even some of these – like shesham wood, which takes twenty years to grow to maturity – are not being replanted fast enough. It's great to provide an unemployed carver with work, or give him decent wages so he can afford to send his children to school, but it's also vital that we look to the future. Will the materials needed be readily available then?

Asha Handicrafts is taking environmental issues very seriously. It has set up a new forestry project which will ensure the long-term availability of raw materials for its woodcarvers, and help to protect the environment too. "What we take from the environment," says Mary Fernandes of Asha, "we need to return to it. Deforestation is very harmful; it can bring about unwanted climatic changes, affecting man. The effects of climate change are already evident. We need to act now."

She also points out other benefits provided by trees, "they reduce city noise, improve habitats for wildlife, provide medicines, provide shade in summer and shelter in winter. They help disperse rainfall over a more even area, and absorb water, thus preventing flooding and helping to retain topsoil. Fallen leaves keep moisture close to the ground, aiding growth and trapping chemicals, keeping them out of lakes and rivers. Locally, they help keep communities healthy. Globally, they maintain our environment in ways we are only just beginning to understand – their chief benefit being to absorb carbon dioxide and mitigate the effects of global warming."

Asha's new project will include purchasing the land, managing the trees, and raising awareness, especially amongst children, about the environment. Demand for wood is outstripping supply in India, and Asha wants to involve the Worldwide Fund for Nature and the Global Forest and Trade Network, who are collaborating on a scheme which can be recognised by the FSC.

I am keen to promote Asha's project, and Shared Earth is donating profits from sales of paper bags to buy more land and plant more trees. We also intend to offset our carbon emissions, initially for travel, by making further donations, and want to encourage other organisations to contribute to this or similar projects as a way of off-setting their own emissions. Whilst many people feel that carbon off-setting is insufficient, it is, I believe, better than doing nothing.

Asha's scheme will benefit everyone. From the purchase of the initial seeds through to the planting of saplings, the management of the forest and the felling of the trees, everything – even the transportation of the wood to the carvers – will be governed by fair trade standards. But what is the problem? Is it the way trade works, or the way the environment is being harmed? With resources running out, is over-consumption overtaking unfair trade as the key issue we need to address? Whichever problem comes first – trade or environment – won't be such an issue if more projects like Asha's get under way.

Fairness is key to dealing with problems of over-consumption and climate change; we in the First World need to take more responsibility for the effects our lifestyles have on people across the globe. Fair trade has much to offer. We need to go on expanding the products we can offer consumers – whether it's coffins, cats or fair trade sex toys!

In the 1950s, every housewife went out with a shopping bag. Then they gave them up and used plastic bags instead. Now they're going back to re-usable bags again. Is this a sacrifice? The way we adapted in the Second World War – and were happy to do so – shows how people can easily adapt their habits.

When I opened Shared Earth in 1986 – or rather, One World, as it was called at the time – most shops put your purchases straight into a bag, without asking if you wanted one. This was anathema to me. I was determined that we should set a better example, and gained a reputation for being a stickler on this issue. It even affected my customer care. Apparently, I used to smile at customers who said they didn't want a bag, and frown at them if they said they did.

Our attitudes towards the use of plastic bags are an indicator of attitudes towards the environment in general. I recently asked a group of schoolchildren how many plastic bags they thought we used in Britain each year.

"Ten million?" asked one.

"At least fifty million," said another.

"Five hundred million!" said an eight-year old boy audaciously.

"I'm afraid none of you are even close," I told them. "The answer – believe it or not –is thirteen *billion*."

Plastic bags are used, on average, for twenty minutes, and then thrown away. They litter our countryside, and over a million seabirds and sea animals lost their lives last year, their wings, beaks or legs caught in plastic, or their digestive tracts blocked because the plastic was mistaken for food.

In Ireland, a bag tax introduced in 2002 reduced usage by 90%. In many other countries, measures are in place to restrict usage or ban them completely. Two years ago designer Anya Hindmarch brought the issue to the headlines in the UK when she released her cotton shopper, priced £5, with the logo 'I'm Not a Plastic Bag.' It sold out within an hour and soon was fetching £200 on eBay.

On 27 February 2008 the Daily Mail launched its 'Banish the Bags' campaign. The next day Marks and Spencer announced that it would start charging 5p per bag in all its stores, and the day after that Prime Minister Gordon Brown became involved, giving retailers a year to introduce charges or be compelled to do so by law. Will he follow this up?

Tesco, the UK's largest retailer, opposes change. It gives out three billion bags a year, and its voluntary scheme to reduce usage by 25% by 2008 was a flop. Sainsbury's, which gives out 1.6 billion bags, also still hands them out free. Sometimes, a box of eggs or a packet of fish have an extra bag all to themselves.

Yet the vast majority of consumers either support the introduction of charges or want an outright ban on plastic bags. The successful bag tax in Ireland proves that it's easy to live without them. According to Wastewatch, a levy would reduce usage by *11 billion* bags each year. The saving of space in landfill sites, and in the lives of animals, would be dramatic.

The reaction to charges at Shared Earth was positive, and bag use dropped dramatically straight away.

"Of *course* I want a bag," said one customer in our York shop, when asked if she wanted one.

"We're charging 10p now," she was told, "I hope that's okay?"

"Oh, I see. Well, maybe I can do without it," she said, pulling an empty carrier out of her pocket.

Another customer was having a bad hair day.

"Would you like a bag?" she was asked.

"Compared to *what?*" she said angrily. Like any other retailer, the patience of our staff is tested daily by the great British public.

Fortunately, there are encouraging signs that attitudes are changing. Bit by bit, we are accepting our responsibility to the world we live in. Developing counties are often ahead of us in realising what needs to be done – and we can learn from them. Some of the best new products coming on the market are made with recycled materials. On my last trip abroad, almost every one of our suppliers was developing exciting new ranges. Old wedding dresses, broken bangles and even camel dung were being converted into marketable gifts.

In Bangladesh, cement, rice and sugar sacks have long been converted into shopping bags. It's a poor country and people can't afford waste; I didn't see one person using a plastic bag there. Now they're exporting cement bag shoppers to Europe.

Motif, one of Shared Earth's most recent suppliers, has taken the art of recycling even further. Its workshop in Kalibari, a village three hours north of Dhaka, employs up to a hundred people, producing a variety of recycled and sustainable products. Crisp packets are their speciality. After washing them several times in water, they cut them into lengths and wind them round strips of bamboo. These are then woven into baskets, place-mats, shopping bags, mobiles, picture frames and office accessories, using traditional weaving techniques. This creates a wonderful mosaic of colour that's more attractive to the eye than any other plastic product.

Motif is very different from our first supplier, Crafts of Africa, which exports Kisii stone from Kenya. Paul Wahome, its founder, is from Nairobi and was one of the first producers to visit us in York. In the evening, I tried to show him round the city; I thought he would like to see its old streets and buildings. However, he was obviously not listening to a word I said. We got as far as King's Square, which is about two minutes' walk from our shop. Suddenly, he lunged out; there was a commotion and a flapping of wings. Next minute, there he was, grinning, holding a frightened pigeon in his hands.

"It has a broken leg," he said. "We need to look after it."

I had not anticipated spending our evening together trying to splint a pigeon's leg, but fair trade leads you, at times, into some strange situations.

Fair trade is about caring for people and our planet. It's a worldwide movement which benefits, above all, producers who are struggling to make a living. So it's only fitting that Paul, who was brought up in a Nairobi slum, should have the last word.

He's written a poem specifically for this book. It's not about sex toys, though. Sorry about that.

"Fair trade is an attitude of mind.
Fair trade is an attitude of heart.
Fair trade is here to stay.
Long live fair trade! Long live fair trade!"

Acknowledgements

So many people have helped me to write this book by telling me their stories, sharing their thoughts and providing information that it's hard to know where to start. They include Richard Adams, Agung Alit, Andy Atkins, Chakkali Bal, Sarvari Begum, Milan Bhattarai, Lucas Caldeira, Paul Chandler, Lynne Dawson, Benny Dembitzer, Jagwati Devi, Rachel Farey, Mo Fini, Christine Ghent, Gulfam, Les Harper, Bhawna Jain, Ravi Jayawardena, Bob Jones, Bone Jones, Padam Kapoor, Modestus Karunaratne, Fulmaya Lama, Harriet Lamb, James Lloyd, Jacqui McDonald, Malcolm Metyard, Ruth Minich, Mary Murata, Mark Patchett, Alison Piercy, Liz Piercy, Neil Rafisura, John Riches, Roy Scott, Dev Sethi, George Shand, Moon Sharma, Kath Shortley, Sue Smith, Stephen Thomas, Paul Wahome, William Wainman, Carol Wills, and Laura Wilson.

Special thanks go to those who have worked with me on the script. My publisher, Adam Kirkman, has been terrific, contributing editor Nick Witt has made many excellent suggestions, whilst Andrew Carter and Anna Ludlow have given me some very useful advice. Michelle Hughes, Shared Earth's head designer, has helped me to prepare the photos.

Thank you, too, to all Shared Earth's suppliers, staff and customers. Fair trade is growing, and all of you are playing a valuable part in making it successful and better known. Long live fair trade!

Index